CW00431770

THE FLIGHT

A PHOTOGRAPHIC JOURNAL CELEBRATING THE BATTLE OF BRITAIN MEMORIAL FLIGHT – WITH RAF AIRCREW STORIES FROM WORLD WAR II

BY JOHN M. DIBBS

& SQN LDR CLIVE ROWLEY MBE

KEY PUBLISHING

Publisher and Managing Director:
Adrian Cox

Executive Chairman:
Richard Cox

Commercial Director:
Ann Saundry

Group Editor:
Nigel Price

Editor:
Allan Burney

All air-to-air colour photography:
© John M. Dibbs

Concept and design:
© John M. Dibbs and Allan Burney

Layout and pre-production:
John M. Dibbs and Philip Hempell

Production:
The Plane Picture Company and Narcosis Media

Production managers:
Iain Dougall and Brian Denesen

www.planepicture.com (www.facebook.com/theplanepicture)

Distribution:
Crécy Publishing, 1a Ringway Trading Estate, Shadowmoss Rd, Manchester, M22 5LH. Tel +44 (0) 1614 990024

Printing:
Gwasg Gomer Cyf/Gomer Press Ltd, Parc Menter Llandysul, Llandysul, Ceredigion SA44 4JL. Tel +44 (0) 1559 362371

Published by Key Publishing Ltd,
PO Box 100, Stamford, Lincs PE19 1XQ.
Tel: +44 (0) 1780 755131. Fax: +44 (0) 1780 757261.
Website: www.keypublishing.com

ISBN (UK): 978 1 912205 26 4

EB G
P7350
IS YOUR OXYGEN
CYLINDER TURNED ON?
DO NOT FORGET
TO CHECK
PULL DOWN STEP
JX B
LF363
OIL
9 GALLS
AIRSPACE
1½ GALLS

INTRODUCTION

JOHN M. DIBBS: PHOTOGRAPHER

The Royal Air Force played a huge part in defining the world we live in today. The battles over Britain during the summer of 1940 changed the course of the war as the RAF inflicted the first defeat on Hitler's war machine. Spitfires and Hurricanes duelled with Messerschmitts and Heinkels until the planned invasion and final piece of Hitler's European domination was deemed too costly to complete and was 'postponed indefinitely'. From that point the fight was taken from the shores of the UK to the Continent, spearheaded by the RAF's Bomber Command which fought many famous tactical and strategic campaigns to bring about the end of the war. Over D-Day in 1944, Spitfires were still fighting back the enemy to afford protection for bombers and ground troops. The actions of those years became the stuff of legend.

However the cost in lives was tremendous, and such a sacrifice cannot be ignored. That is why The Battle of Britain Memorial Flight is so important and precious. It seeks to commemorate the loss and celebrate those who survived, not only in World War 2, but also in conflicts since.

It truly is an honour to photograph and fly with the BBMF, they are a testament to the skill and professionalism of those who serve. Since my earliest flights, I have wanted to produce a book that reflects today's RAF, but also provides a platform to the veterans' voices and memories. Ordinary people called upon to become extraordinary warriors. Their stories, brought to life by the skill of Sqn Ldr Clive Rowley, are inspiring, thought provoking, humorous and tragic. It is my hope that this book captures a little of their defiant spirit, real people fighting a real war. 'The Flight' is a celebration of their lives and is dedicated to them.

SQN LDR CLIVE ROWLEY MBE: AUTHOR

According to my mother, I was seven years old when I first announced that I was going to be a fighter pilot when I grew up. Later, after seeing a Spitfire in the air for the first time, I dreamed of flying one of these beautiful and charismatic machines. I am extremely fortunate to have achieved both of these far-fetched ambitions. I flew jet fighters with the RAF from 1972 until 2003, and displayed the Spitfires and Hurricanes of the RAF Battle of Britain Memorial Flight for 11 years.

My time with the RAF and especially with the BBMF has given me the privileged opportunity of meeting many veteran pilots and aircrew who flew operationally during World War 2 in far more dangerous circumstances than I ever faced. The conversations I have had with them, their stoic sense of duty, their modesty and their understated but incredible stories have left an indelible impression on me.

When John Dibbs asked me if I would like to contribute to this book, it didn't take me long to realise that this was something that I should do. With John's brilliant and beautiful photographs, this book is a celebration of the BBMF, 'The Flight' of the title. However, when John explained his concept to me, I realised that it would also be a commemoration of those courageous individuals who went to war in these aircraft, something that is fundamental to the BBMF's ethos with its motto 'Lest we forget'. With snapshots of their exploits told in their own words, not only can we gain an insight into the remarkable things they did and the trials and tribulations they faced, but we also get a sense of their innate modesty in the unheroic style of their telling. Let there be no misunderstanding though, these were true heroes.

Foreword by:
His Royal Highness Prince William
The Duke of Cambridge KG KT ADC(P)
Patron of the Royal Air Force
Battle of Britain Memorial Flight

KENSINGTON PALACE

As patron of the Royal Air Force Battle of Britain Memorial Flight it gives me great pleasure to write this foreword on the occasion of the Flight's Sixtieth Anniversary.

There are few sights or sounds that evoke a more emotional response than a display or flypast by the iconic aircraft of the BBMF. They tug at the heart strings, bringing many to tears; they generate a sense of pride, lifting the spirits of veterans and the public alike and they inspire all those who see them. The Flight's aircraft provide a living tribute of the nation's respect for all who those who have served with the Royal Air Force across the generations; especially those who have lost their lives fighting to preserve the freedom of others.

Sixty years on from the Flight's inception in 1957 the BBMF's historic aircraft are maintained and flown to the same exacting standards as the most modern aircraft in the Royal Air Force. The aircrew and engineers operate these aircraft with the same professionalism, dedication and selflessness of those who went before them, in far more dangerous circumstances during World War Two. In those six decades the BBMF has displayed or flown past at thousands of events, including State occasions and major commemorations. The Flight has become a household name and a national institution. With its synthesis of old and modern, then and now, the BBMF represents a continuance of the core values of the Royal Air Force; professional excellence, teamwork and selflessness.

The next time that you see the BBMF aircraft, apart from marvelling at the sheer spectacle and symphonic sound, please recognise the tribute offered to all those who have died serving in the Royal Air Force and, at the same time, spare a thought for those who continue to serve today.

FOREWORD

Thursday 11 July 1957. Three ex-Battle of Britain pilots including Group Captain Peter Thompson DFC, fly three Mark XIX Spitfires from RAF Woodvale to RAF Biggin Hill. Their arrival at that most famous of stations marked the birth of what we now know as the Battle of Britain Memorial Flight.

Two of those founding aircraft are still on the Flight today, stalwart members of the RAF's most exclusive unit. They join four other Spitfires, two Hurricanes, two Chipmunks, the Dakota and, the jewel in the crown, the Lancaster.

Who better to record these most beautiful aircraft than the world-renowned photographer and author John Dibbs? The images in this book are truly stunning and capture the grace, beauty and raw power of these fantastic flying machines. John's attention to detail and unique composition has captured the Flight's aircraft at their most striking.

The sedate elegance of the Dakota, the bullish, purposeful no-nonsense lines of the Hurricane, the sheer size and might of the Lancaster and, of course, the unmistakeable curves of the Spitfire, surely the most beautiful flying machine and weapon ever designed. They represent a spectacular and visceral link to this island's venerable history. An island whose people and those from her dominions, were lone defenders of civilisation in the early years of the war. These aircraft and their ilk, flown by young men many barely out of .their teens, ensured the eventual turning of the tide against National Socialist tyranny. These aircraft were the only way the fight could be taken to the enemy's front door.

As the Royal Air Force's BBMF enters its 60th year, it is most fitting to reflect on the sacrifice of all those who have lost or given their lives whilst in the service of this fine country.

There still remain a number of veterans of those days, men who flew these machines and risked all for generations not yet born. Many more have passed on and many lost their lives fighting for our freedom. It is to commemorate them that the BBMF exists. This book marks their contribution in the best way possible, their amazing feats glimpsed through their own understated words, collated by former OC BBMF, Clive Rowley. Dibbs' beautiful photographs coupled with historical images enrich their remarkable stories.

This is a spectacular way to mark the Flight's 60th anniversary. I am hopeful that the Flight's aircraft will still be flying as a living memorial in another 60 years' time.

Lest We Forget.

SQN LDR ANDY 'MILLI' MILLIKIN RAF
THE OFFICER COMMANDING
THE RAF BATTLE OF BRITAIN MEMORIAL FLIGHT

FOREWORD

SQN LDR GEORGE 'JOHNNY' JOHNSON MBE DFM

It is a great privilege to be asked to write the foreword for a book which deals with one unit's remembrance of the Royal Air Force's contribution to the winning of the Second World War.

Throughout its 60 years the Battle of Britain Memorial Flight has kept alive the memory of how, whilst Fighter Command defended this country in the Battle of Britain, Bomber Command carried the fight to Europe itself. The Spitfire and Hurricane still show that fighter spirit in their swift manoeuvres and the power of the Lancaster upholds the Bomber Command pride.

It is the Lancaster with which I am most familiar. I spent two years of my war in the nose of one of these magnificent machines. The Lancaster was the greatest four engined heavy bomber of World War 2. It was completely reliable and capable of carrying a much heavier bomb load than its 'colleagues'. The 'music' of those four Merlin engines still reawakens the feelings of tremendous pride in its performance.

My personal experience attests to the ability of the aircraft to be recovered from a lightning strike after falling 8,000ft in a few seconds and to be flown on the two starboard engines and still land politely. Both of these activities depend, of course, on the skill and ability of the pilot and I consider myself to have been extremely fortunate to have flown with one who had these skills aplenty.

For most of my operational time I was the bomb aimer on Flight Lieutenant Joe McCarthy's crew. Joe was an American in the Canadian Air Force, 6ft 3in tall and with the breadth to go with it! Big in size, big in personality and big in pilot ability. I was lucky enough to be on his crew when Wing Commander Gibson asked if he would like to join a special squadron that was being formed for one specific trip. Joe asked the crew if they were willing, which we were, and hence began our involvement in the 'Dams Raid'. Much has been written, filmed and televised about this, so I will limit my account to my personal memories.

Firstly, there was the specially modified Lancaster. The mid-upper turret had been removed and the bomb bay doors had apparently been sealed. Just behind the nose, on either side of the fuselage, two legs were sticking down, one of which had a small bevelled wheel attached. When the bomb arrived, their function was apparent – it was like a glorified, galvanised dustbin that would be carried perfectly by the two legs.

Training was exhilarating as it concentrated on low flying ie 100ft was the brief, in practice it was nearer 60. For us however, the actual delivery of the bomb would not be as we trained. We were sent to the Sorpe Dam and the position in the hills meant that we would not get a straight run up to it and there were no towers for me to train my sights on. We were briefed to fly along the dam with the port outer engine over the dam itself and estimate the centre point to release the bomb. This would not be an easy task as if we missed the mid-point Joe would have to pull up immediately to avoid the hills on the other side. If I was not satisfied with the position, I would say 'Dummy Run' and if Joe wasn't happy he would just pull up. The lower the aircraft was the less forward travel there would be before the bomb hit the surface. On the tenth run we were at 30ft. As I said 'Bomb Gone', there was an appreciative, if irreverent, comment from the rear gunner.

Unfortunately, not enough aircraft got through to the Sorpe to crack it, but we had the satisfaction of knowing that we had done enough damage to warrant the dam being drained for repair.

Left: The crew of Lancaster ED285/AJ-T. Left to right: Sgt George Johnson, bomb aimer; PO Donald A. MacLean, navigator; Flt Lt Joseph C. McCarthy, pilot; Sgt Leonard Eaton, gunner. At the rear are Sgt Ronald Batson, front gunner; and Sgt William G. Ratcliffe, flight engineer.

HW R

We suffered terrible losses. Of the 16 aircraft that got over the North Sea only eight returned. Fifty three men lost their lives and three were taken prisoner. This was a tragic loss for one squadron on one operation. However, we achieved two thirds of our objective, the dams were breached and production of steel on the Ruhr was severely interrupted and labour had to be withdrawn from other areas to make the repairs. Most importantly, it was a huge morale boost for war torn Britain as it proved that Bomber Command could penetrate the heart of Germany.

The Lancaster continued to prove her worth throughout the rest of the war with punishing raids over land and sea, the sinking of the *Tirpitz*, followed by humanitarian raids like Operation 'Manna'.

All the aircraft that fly in the BBMF are special, but my favourite is the Lancaster and its musical four Merlin engines. From its formation, the BBMF has flown hundreds of operations, from Trooping of the Colour to air shows and international events. It represents the pride and respect that the British public have for the Royal Air Force and its history. For me the most impressive flypast was over the site of the International Bomber Command Centre, with the last flying Vulcan, although 'Thumper's' double act with 'Vera' during the summer of 2014 was also outstanding.

This is a very special book of John Dibbs' magnificent photos and Clive Rowley's veteran stories that commemorate those that served and celebrates the fantastic work of the BBMF. Keep the Merlins singing lads and the Lancaster in the air.

GL (Johnny) Johnson
617 Sqn

'It's nice to be remembered, because being remembered covers everybody, including all those chaps who were killed. That's what's important, not medals or thanks.'

Squadron Leader Geoffrey Wellum DFC

CONTENTS

16 THE FLIGHT IS BORN

22 THE BBMF TODAY

28 THE AIRCRAFT

30 SPITFIRE P7350

50 SPITFIRE AB910

68 DAKOTA ZA947

80 HURRICANE LF363

102 SPITFIRE MK356

112 SPITFIRE PM631 & PS915

122 LANCASTER PA474

154 SPITFIRE TE311

158 HURRICANE PZ865

178 CHIPMUNK WG486 & WK518

180 KEEPING THE DREAM ALIVE

188 APPENDICES

YB W
RF D

THE FLIGHT IS BORN

The Royal Air Force Battle of Britain Memorial Flight (RAF BBMF) was founded at a formal ceremony held at RAF Biggin Hill, the famous Battle of Britain airfield in Kent, on 11 July 1957. The unit was unveiled as the Historic Aircraft Flight, although it was already being referred to, not least in the RAF Biggin Hill Operational Record (F540) for that day, as the Battle of Britain Flight, a name which became its official title just a few months later in February 1958.

'FOUNDING FATHER'

The driving force behind the foundation of the Flight – the 'founding father' – was Gp Capt Peter D. Thompson DFC, although he would have been embarrassed to be referred to as such. At the time he was the Station Commander at RAF Biggin Hill, but his motivation in forming the Flight was not in the least self-serving. Instead, it was driven entirely by his strongly-held belief that the vital importance of the RAF's victory in the Battle of Britain should continue to be commemorated with aircraft of the principal RAF types that participated – the Hurricane and Spitfire – and that those who served with the RAF, and especially the many who sacrificed their lives fighting against tyranny during World War 2, should be remembered. His own version of the part he played, written in a letter to the BBMF in 1999, was simply to say: 'I did have a hand in collecting together the aircraft that in due time formed the nucleus of what is now the Battle of Britain Memorial Flight'.

Peter Thompson was himself an ex-wartime RAF fighter pilot who had joined the RAF Volunteer Reserve in January 1939, aged 18. He flew Hawker Hurricanes during the final weeks of the Battle of Britain with No 605 Squadron Auxiliary Air Force and subsequently in Malta with Nos 261 and 185 Squadrons from April 1941 to January 1942. After one combat he was forced to bale out of his Hurricane over Malta at very low level, so low in fact that both he and his aircraft landed in the same field. 'A close run thing', he said. After his return to the UK he was awarded the Distinguished Flying Cross (DFC). In 1943, after a period as an instructor and then as a test pilot in the Middle East, he served as a flight commander with No 601 Squadron AuxAF, flying Spitfires in North Africa, Sicily and Italy. After returning to the UK he took command of No 129 Squadron in July 1944, a position he held until April 1945. Operating from RAF Ford, flying North American P-51 Mustang Mk IIIs, he destroyed three V-1 flying bombs and damaged two more. His final wartime 'tally' was three enemy aircraft destroyed (plus three V-1s), two shared destroyed, two probably destroyed and four (plus two V-1s) damaged.

Post war Peter Thompson remained in the RAF on a permanent commission and flew Gloster Meteor and Hawker Hunter jet fighters. Peacetime military flying was not without its risks and he had to abandon an aircraft for the second time in his career when the tail of his Meteor was knocked off in a mid-air collision with an American F-86 Sabre; he landed by parachute in Guildford High Street. In 1955 he was posted to RAF Biggin Hill as the Wing Commander Flying and then in 1956 became the Station Commander when it became a Wing Commander Station.

FOUNDING AIRCRAFT

Obviously, there could be no Historic Aircraft Flight without the historic aircraft, specifically Spitfires and Hurricanes.

Hurricane LF363, which had been retained somewhat unofficially by the RAF, was now the only airworthy example of its type in RAF hands. Having recently been overhauled by Hawker and Rolls-Royce free of charge, it was now on the strength of the Station Flight at Biggin Hill, designated as an 'Exhibition Aircraft' on its record card and available to form the nucleus of the new Historic Flight. It is probably true to say that without the existence of LF363 in flying condition, the BBMF would never have existed. This famous old Hurricane is still flying with the BBMF, although not without incident during the intervening years.

Above: The 'founding father' of the BBMF, Gp Capt Peter D. Thompson DFC.

Left: The three most iconic types operated by the BBMF, Spitfire, Hurricane and Lancaster.

Sourcing Spitfires for the new Flight was more problematic. Spitfires had already been withdrawn from RAF service and the only examples still flying in the UK were three photo-reconnaissance PR Mk XIXs of the civilian-operated Temperature and Humidity (THUM) Flight at Woodvale, Lancashire. These last remaining airworthy Spitfires were also about to be retired and grounded. Rather than let that happen, it was decided that these Mk XIXs – PM631, PS853 and PS915 – would be allocated to the Historic Aircraft Flight. The Spitfires were flown from Woodvale to RAF Duxford. They were due to be delivered on 12 June, but perhaps indicative of the state the aircraft were in, PS915 went unserviceable with an engine problem and PS853 suffered an engine failure on take-off and ended up 'taking a header into the ground', to quote a contemporary newspaper report. The three aircraft eventually made it to Duxford after the necessary rectification and repairs.

11 JULY 1957

The three Spitfires were flown from Duxford to Biggin Hill to form the new Flight on 11 July 1957. The three-ship formation was led by the RAF's highest scoring fighter ace of World War 2, Gp Capt J. E. 'Johnnie' Johnson DSO and two Bars DFC and Bar (later Air Vice Marshal CB CBE DSO and two bars DFC and Bar) flying Spitfire PR Mk XIX PS853. Another famous, high-scoring RAF fighter ace, Gp Capt (later Air Commodore) James Rankin DSO and Bar DFC and Bar, flew PM631, one of his last and surely his most pleasurable duties before he retired from the RAF in 1958. As the most junior of the trio, Peter Thompson was left to fly PS915, which the others felt was not in the best shape! (In fact this was subsequently confirmed, as PS915 was retired from flying duties almost immediately and remained grounded until 1986. It eventually re-joined the BBMF in April 1987 and still serves with the Flight.)

Above left: During their delivery flight to Biggin Hill, the Spitfires were escorted by a Hunter and Javelin.

Left: Air Marshal Sir Thomas Pike KCB CBE DFC and Bar, formally creates the Historic Aircraft Flight at Biggin Hill on 11 July 1957.

Right: The three Spitfire PR Mk XIXs at Woodvale.

Below right: Thompson, Rankin and Johnson (left to right) at Biggin Hill on 11 July 1957.

En route to Biggin Hill the three Spitfires were met and escorted by three Hawker Hunter F5s of No 41 Squadron from Biggin Hill and three Gloster Javelins of No 46 Squadron from RAF Odiham.

On arrival at Biggin Hill at 11:00 hours, the trio were greeted by the Air Officer Commanding-in-Chief of Fighter Command, Air Marshal Sir Thomas Pike KCB CBE DFC and Bar. At a ceremony held on the airfield, with Spitfire PS853 providing a backdrop, the AOC-in-C formally announced the formation of the Historic Aircraft Flight. The BBMF had been born!

EARLY DAYS

Peter Thompson had gained the necessary high-level approval to form the new Flight, but it was made clear to him that there would be no public funding and no established manpower for the maintenance and operation of the historic aircraft. The Flight was to be operated on an entirely voluntary basis. He approached his OC Engineering Wing at Biggin Hill, Sqn Ldr E. H. Sowden (later Wg Cdr Sowden MBE), who had worked as an RAF engineer on Hurricanes and Spitfires during the war, and asked for his help. In addition to his 'day job' of organising the maintenance of the Station's Hawker Hunters, Sowden assembled and led a team of suitably experienced volunteer tradesmen to work on the Flight's historic aircraft.

Peter Thompson and others were not entirely happy that the only Spitfires available to the Flight were unarmed photo-reconnaissance versions, not at all representative of the fighter variants of the Spitfire. Somehow, he persuaded the authorities to allocate three Mk XVI Spitfires to the Flight from storage. These Spitfires were regarded purely as ground demonstration aircraft, but he believed that they could be made airworthy relatively easily. Sqn Ldr Sowden agreed and he also knew that spares were more readily available for the Mk XVIs. He prioritised work on the Mk XVIs and the first to fly was TE330, which was air tested by Peter Thompson in September 1957.

PETER THOMPSON'S LEGACY

By 1958, when Peter Thompson was posted away from Biggin Hill, the Battle of Britain Flight consisted of Hurricane LF363, Spitfire Mk XVIs TE330, TE476 and SL674, and Spitfire PR Mk XIX PM631. He left the Flight on a firm footing and laid the foundations for its subsequent growth to the established unit that is so well-known and loved today. The RAF and the millions of people who see the BBMF aircraft still flying today owe an unknown debt of gratitude to Peter Thompson for his foresight and determination in founding the Flight in 1957.

Peter Thompson's final appointment in the RAF was as Air Attaché at the British Embassy in Lima, in Peru. He retired as a group captain in September 1975 and settled in Menorca. In 1998 he was invited to visit the BBMF at RAF Coningsby and was delighted to find the BBMF still operating over 41 years after he set it up, and as an established unit with its own hangar. 'No longer tucked away in a cluttered corner of the Station Flight hangar, but a proud display in immaculate surroundings', as he said. 'Thoroughbreds every one', he went on, 'even Spitfire XIX PS915, which I flew into Biggin Hill over 40 years before… it and the others in splendid condition.'

Peter Thompson passed away on 2 March 2003, aged 82, but his legacy, the Battle of Britain Memorial Flight, lives on.

Left: Early BBMF fighter formation.

Right: Spitfire and Hurricane break.

LF363

GN
F

THE BBMF TODAY

From its beginnings in 1957 as a rather 'rag-bag' collection of obsolete aircraft, without any official funding and with an entirely volunteer workforce, the Royal Air Force Battle of Britain Memorial Flight (RAF BBMF) has evolved into a regular, supported RAF unit, funded by the Ministry of Defence and manned by established, full-time Service personnel supporting its fleet of 12 historic aircraft. The BBMF has also become a household name and a national institution. It is estimated that over 7 million people see the BBMF aircraft at the various events they attend during the display season each year.

PRESERVING AND COMMEMORATING

The long-term preservation of the BBMF historic aircraft in airworthy condition is a fundamental aim of the modern BBMF. Those entrusted with this responsibility are well aware that these aircraft are priceless artefacts of the RAF's heritage and today they are flown carefully and maintained to a far higher standard than was possible when they flew operationally in wartime. The BBMF personnel believe passionately that the aircraft should be kept where they belong, in the air, as a living memorial to those who have gone before. This is no easy task and requires long-term planning, as well as careful husbandry of the aircraft by limiting g-loadings, maximum speeds, engine power settings and the number of flying hours on the aircraft for each display season.

The BBMF's commemorative role is perhaps its most important purpose. Although the Flight was originally formed to commemorate the RAF airmen who died during World War 2 and particularly during the Battle of Britain, it now flies in tribute to all those who have lost their lives in service with the RAF or its predecessor the Royal Flying Corps (RFC), in all conflicts from 1914 up to the present day. Over 100,000 RFC or RAF personnel have been killed in service: 9,352 during World War 1, 70,253 during World War 2, and over 16,000 since. The BBMF reminds us all of the debt we owe to those who have paid the ultimate price in the service of their country, fighting to preserve the freedom of others.

Aside from these cornerstones of the BBMF's existence, the Flight also aims to promote the RAF and its heritage by displaying its aircraft on the ground and in the air on as many occasions as possible, demonstrating to the public that the RAF is proud of its heritage and that the modern Service strives to maintain the same sense of duty, dedication, professionalism and skill now, as was evident when these aircraft flew operationally.

Finally, the BBMF aims to inspire all those who see its aircraft flying, especially the younger generation, to share the passion of all RAF aircrew to fly and the commitment of all RAF personnel who serve the country. There are, after all, few sights or sounds able to provoke more powerful emotions than that of the BBMF aircraft.

THE BBMF AIRCRAFT FLEET

The BBMF fleet now consists of a total of 12 airworthy aircraft and includes one of only two flying Avro Lancaster four-engine heavy bombers in the world. A C-47 Dakota represents the dogged work of the military transport aircraft and crews. The Flight's six Supermarine Spitfires range from a 1940 Mk IIa – the only surviving, flying Spitfire from the Battle of Britain – through a Mk Vb, a Mk IX, a Mk XVI and two photo-reconnaissance PR Mk XIXs. The Flight also proudly holds on its strength two Hawker Hurricanes of 1944 vintage, including the last Hurricane ever built, PZ865, the 'Last of the Many'. Finally, two de Havilland Chipmunk T10 training aircraft make up the full complement. Some of the BBMF aircraft have remarkable wartime histories of their own and most have defied the odds to survive as flying examples of their kind. Three of the aircraft, Hurricane LF363 and PR Mk XIX Spitfires PM631 and PS915, were founder members of the Flight in 1957. The carefully researched and authentic colour schemes applied to the BBMF aircraft tell stories of amazing and inspirational human endeavour.

Left: Hurricane LF363 and Spitfire P7350 marked up as the aircraft of Tom Neil and Geoffrey Wellum respectively.

EB
G
P7350

BBMF AIRCREW

The majority of the pilots and aircrews who fly the BBMF aircraft are volunteers, as they have been since the Flight's formation in 1957. They have other primary duties elsewhere within the RAF and fly the BBMF aircraft mainly in their own time; a privilege but also a considerable personal commitment.

There are only two full-time officers and pilots on the Flight, the Officer Commanding (OC BBMF), a squadron leader post, and the Operations Officer, a flight lieutenant, both of whom are fighter pilots by trade.

The Officer Commanding is responsible for overseeing all the operations, public relations, administration and engineering functions on the Flight, and for the overall planning and management of the display programme. He also holds the role of Fighter Leader, responsible for training BBMF fighter pilots and for conducting air tests on the BBMF fighter aircraft. In order to ensure continuity and a succession plan, each OC BBMF is preselected for the post and serves as a volunteer fighter pilot with the Flight for four years to build up the necessary experience before taking command of the BBMF for a three-year tour of duty.

The BBMF Operations Officer, meanwhile, is responsible for the detailed planning and management of the extensive display programme undertaken by the Flight every year and for the necessary liaison with event organisers. The display programme takes careful and extensive planning and co-ordination, not least because each sortie usually involves several events to maximise the opportunities within the limited aircraft flying hours available.

The BBMF Spitfires and Hurricanes are flown by RAF fighter pilots, of whom there are normally six on the team, including the OC BBMF and the BBMF Operations Officer.

The Dakota and Lancaster are flown by RAF pilots with a background on heavy, multi-engine, multi-crew aircraft and they bring those skill-sets to the BBMF. There are normally three Lancaster/Dakota captains on the Flight and two Dakota captain/ Lancaster co-pilots.

The BBMF's volunteer navigators, flight engineers and air loadmasters, who also crew the Lancaster and Dakota, are all essential to the safe and efficient operation of these aircraft and all have other duties within the RAF.

Above: Dakota ZA947 marked as No 233 Squadron's FZ692 Kwicherbichen.

Left: Aircraft of the BBMF fleet on the apron at RAF Coningsby.

BBMF ENGINEERING

The maintenance, to airworthy condition, of the Flight's 12 historic aircraft is the responsibility of the BBMF engineering team, which consists of 30 RAF engineering technicians headed by the Flight's Senior Engineering Officer (a squadron leader). The engineers who make up this relatively small team have all volunteered for duties with the Flight and serve a nominal three to five years tour of duty. A small cadre of full-time-reservist (FTRS) technicians, with long experience in servicing the BBMF historic aircraft, provides on-the-job training to the regular RAF technicians.

THE BBMF YEAR

The BBMF year is split into two, roughly equal halves.

During the winter season – from October to March each year – the majority of the Flight's aircraft (except for the

THUMPER

DHC Chipmunks) are kept on the ground for extensive winter maintenance to prepare them for the next display season and to ensure their long-term preservation. Usually, at least one of the aircraft is scheduled to undergo a 'major' maintenance programme each year, under contract, away from Coningsby.

The display season normally runs from the beginning of May to the end of September each year, with pre-season work-up flying for the crews taking place in April, culminating in Public Display Approval being granted to each pilot by the Air Officer Commanding. During the display season, all the aircraft fly regularly and often deploy away on display duties. Meanwhile, routine servicing and rectification work also takes place in the Flight's hangar. During each display season, the BBMF is typically tasked to fly over 100 displays and around 300-400 flypasts at events of all shapes and sizes, generating around 1,000 individual aircraft appearances each year.

LEST WE FORGET

The BBMF and its aircraft continue to remind and to educate us about our heritage, they exemplify the resilience and spirit in the face of adversity that has defeated even the most serious threats to our freedom and they provide a tangible link between the modern RAF and its illustrious history. The Flight's motto, 'Lest we forget', says it all.

Left: Lancaster PA474 marked up as Thumper Mk III *of No 617 Squadron.*

Right: Engineer's panel of the Lancaster.

THE AIRCRAFT

G

SPITFIRE Mk IIa P7350

Supermarine Spitfire Mk IIa P7350 was the 14th of 11,939 Spitfires that were eventually built at the Castle Bromwich 'Shadow' factory, although it was not, in fact, the 14th delivered to the RAF. First flown by famous test pilot Alex Henshaw in August 1940, it was taken on charge by the RAF on 13 August and was delivered, by Henshaw, to No 6 Maintenance Unit (MU) at Brize Norton four days later, for the fitting of operational equipment.

With the Battle of Britain at its height, P7350 was allocated to No 266 Squadron at Wittering on 6 September 1940 and given the code letters UO-T. Subsequently No 266 Squadron moved to Martlesham Heath and then to Collyweston taking P7350 with it. Then, on 17 October 1940, P7350 was one of 13 Mk IIa Spitfires transferred to No 603 (City of Edinburgh) Squadron (AuxAF) at Hornchurch. The aircraft's code letters were changed to No 603 Squadron codes as XT-W. On 25 October, whilst being flown by Polish pilot Ludwik Martel, P7350 was shot down by a German Bf 109. A cannon shell punched a large hole in the port wing and Martel was wounded by shrapnel in the left side of his body and legs. Despite his injuries Martel managed to fly the aircraft down through 16,000ft of thick cloud, in pain and fighting to stay conscious, to force land in a field near Hastings.

P7350 was dispatched to No 1 Civilian Repair Unit at Cowley on 31 October, where it was repaired. On 7 December it was ready for collection and was flown to No 37 MU at Burtonwood, Lancashire, for service preparation and storage.

The Spitfire's next operational unit was No 616 (County of South Yorkshire) Squadron (AuxAF), based at Tangmere, to which it was issued on 18 March 1941. Then on 10 April it was transferred to No 64 Squadron at Hornchurch. With these units P7350 flew on fighter sweeps over occupied Europe as Fighter Command went on the offensive during 1941. Having seemingly incurred damage from an unknown incident, possibly a landing accident, in August 1941 P7350 was moved to Scottish Aviation Ltd at Prestwick for overhaul and repair.

With higher-performance and better-armed versions of the Spitfire now available, the time had come to withdraw Mk II Spitfires from operational flying and P7350 was issued to the Central Gunnery School at Sutton Bridge on 27 April 1942. Here it spent the next 10 months, suffering another Category B accident (beyond repair on site) on 4 February 1943 and being transferred to Air Services Training Ltd at Hamble for repairs. These were completed by 20 March and, after passing through No 6 MU at Brize Norton again, it was issued to No 57 Operational Training Unit (OTU) at Eshott, Northumberland. The next 12 months of its use as a training machine were uneventful, but on 22 April 1944 another Spitfire taxied into P7350, causing further Category B damage, which once again saw it at Air Services Training Ltd for repairs. Thereafter it was placed in storage at No 39 MU Colerne.

Having survived all its wartime adventures, P7350 was declared surplus to requirements by the Air Ministry in 1947 and a year later it was sold as scrap to Messrs John Dale and Sons Ltd, who paid the princely sum of £25 for the now priceless Spitfire. On realising the historical importance of this venerable aircraft, the company generously presented it to RAF Colerne as a museum piece, where it remained until 1967.

The making of the movie 'Battle of Britain' saw Spitfire P7350 emerge from 20 years of dormancy when it was selected to fly in the film. It was delivered to No 71 MU at Henlow on 3 March 1967 to be overhauled to airworthy standard and on 20 May 1968 it was flown to Duxford for use in aerial sequences in the film.

After filming for the movie was complete, P7350 was allocated to the Battle of Britain Flight, being flown to the Flight's base at Coltishall by Sqn Ldr Tim Mills on 5 November 1968. It has served with the BBMF ever since, the only airworthy Spitfire from the Battle of Britain, a much-admired survivor and precious artefact.

Left: The pride of the BBMF, Battle of Britain veteran Spitfire Mk IIa P7350.

Ludwik Martel

Ludwik Martel escaped from Poland to join the RAF in 1940 and was the youngest Polish fighter pilot to fly in the Battle of Britain. Flying Spitfires with No 603 Squadron he shot down a Messerschmitt Bf 109 in October 1940. When he, himself, was shot down on 25 October his nemesis was probably Hauptmann Walter Adolph, the commanding officer of II./JG26 (his 13th kill). Later, Ludwik joined No 317 Squadron then in March 1943 he was posted to the Middle East to join the Polish Fighting Team; there he destroyed a German Bf 109 and damaged two others. After a further tour of duty in England with No 317 Squadron, flying offensive sweeps over France and ground attack sorties in support of the D-Day operations, he took up a staff appointment in the Polish Air Force HQ. When he was released from the RAF in January 1947 he settled in England. Ludwik died on 25 April 2010 aged 91.

'To survive you have to be good and very lucky'

'After I escaped from Poland and joined the RAF I received 20 hours of flight training in the Spitfire Mk I and I felt that it was the most wonderful aircraft I had ever flown. I learned the English language and the English way of flying in an operational training unit and found it to be a very pleasant experience. That was until I went into combat. The early fighter tactics of the RAF were about the only thing I disagreed with. We were taught to fly in a very close, tight formation. With 12 Spitfires flying that close, it was difficult to look around for the Luftwaffe, let alone keeping an eye on our leader. The Germans called our V-shaped formations "idiotenreihen" which meant "rows of idiots". I certainly felt like one when I got shot down in my Spitfire on 25 October 1940, as I stayed in formation while the Bf 109s attacked from above.

'That day, as we climbed in the very close formation, we were told on the radio that enemy aircraft were nearby. Before we realised it, they came down on the squadron. They shot down three of us and I was one of them. There were bangs, a big hole appeared in the wing from a cannon shell and I was wounded. I didn't try to bale out… I couldn't get the hood open. I had plenty of shrapnel in my left side and I fainted. Fortunately, I got my senses back together and I managed to control the aircraft and to land in a field with the undercarriage up.'

Flight Lieutenant Ludwik Martel, Poland, Silver Cross of Virtuti Militari, Cross of Valour and two bars and Silver Cross of Merit

Jeffrey Quill

Jeffrey Quill needs no introduction as the famous Supermarine Spitfire test pilot. A pre-war RAF fighter pilot, he was released by the Service to begin working for Vickers and Supermarine as a company test pilot in January 1936. He flew the prototype Spitfire K5054 on 26 March 1936. In the summer of 1940 he persuaded Vickers that he could do little more for the Spitfire's development without gaining some first-hand experience of combat, a 'spot of practical' as he put it. The RAF agreed to reinstate him as a flying officer and he joined No 65 (East India) Squadron at Hornchurch on 5 August 1940, spending three weeks with the squadron in the thick of the action during the Battle of Britain, and claiming a Bf 109 and a Heinkel He 111 bomber destroyed. He was then told to put his flying officer's uniform back in mothballs and return to his test pilot duties with Vickers and Supermarine. After the war, Quill frequently flew and displayed Spitfire Mk Vb AB910, which was then owned and operated by Vickers, and he delivered the aircraft to Coltishall to hand it over to the BBMF on 15 September 1965, his last flight in a Spitfire. Jeffrey Quill died in 1996, aged 83.

'…it was high time for Quill to be airborne'

'The whole squadron was just formed up on the ground and waiting Sam's signal to start rolling. I was looking out to my left towards the leading section when I became aware of, rather than actually hearing, a sort of reverberating "crump" behind and to my right. I looked quickly over my right shoulder to see one of the hangar roofs close behind us ascending heavenwards. This was followed by showers of earth and black smoke, then more and louder "crumps". I caught a glimpse through the smoke of what looked like a Me 110 pulling sharply out of a dive and immediately concluded that it was high time for Quill to be airborne. We were being dive bombed. I put my head down, slammed the throttle open and went without further ceremony… As I became airborne I glanced in the mirror and saw nothing but bomb-bursts and showers of earth and smoke immediately behind. I thought I must be the only member of the squadron to have got away. Then I saw a Spitfire, and another and another, emerge through the smoke … Miraculously, the whole squadron got airborne except one whose engine was stopped by bomb blast, although the pilot was uninjured.'

Flying Officer Jeffrey Quill AFC OBE FRAeS, No 65 (East India) Squadron (Hornchurch), operating from Manston 12 August 1940

Eric Lock

Eric Lock served with No 41 Squadron flying Spitfires from June 1940 to July 1941. Modern research shows that he was the highest scoring RAF fighter pilot of the Battle of Britain with 21 enemy aircraft confirmed destroyed, plus eight probably destroyed. In November 1940 he was shot down in air combat and seriously wounded by cannon-shell shrapnel in both legs and one arm. He subsequently spent six months in hospital. After recovering from his injuries and returning to flying, he joined No 611 Squadron as a flight commander. Soon after, on 3 August 1941, he failed to return from a fighter sweep over northern France. It is believed that he was shot down by ground fire in the Pas-de-Calais area, but neither he nor his aircraft have ever been found and he is one of the 20,456 airmen with no known grave commemorated on the Runnymede Memorial in Surrey. Although Eric Lock's war was relatively short – he actually 'faced the enemy' for a period of less than four months – he became and remains one of the RAF's top ten aces of World War 2 with a total score of 26.5 enemy aircraft destroyed. All but three of his tally of victories was achieved with No 41 Squadron in just a few weeks of fighting and, notably, most (18) of his kills were against Bf 109 fighters.

This page and overleaf: Spitfire Mk IIa P7350 wearing the No 41 Squadron code letters EB-G, representing the Spitfire Mk I that Eric Lock flew on 5 September 1940, a day when he claimed three enemy aircraft destroyed.

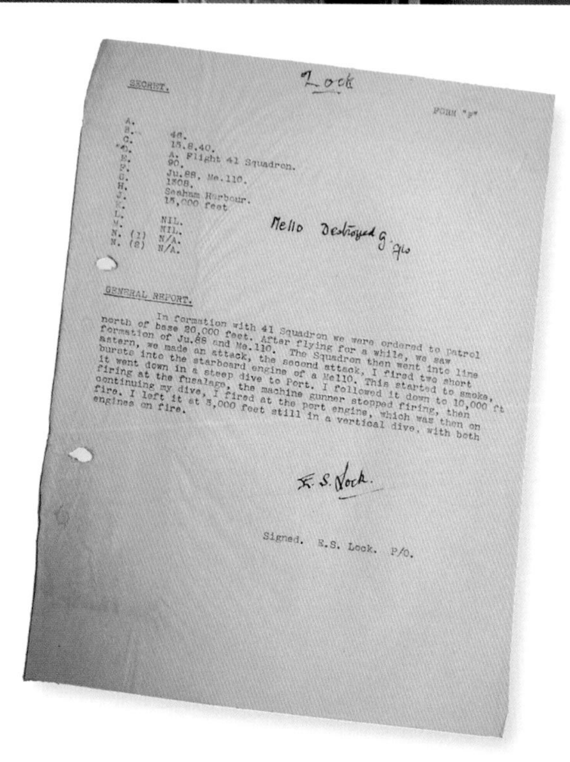

Lock

SECRET.

FORM "F"

A.
B. 46.
C. 15.8.40.
D. A. Flight 41 Squadron.
E. 90.
F. Ju.88. Me.110.
G. 1308.
H. Seaham Harbour.
J. 15,000 feet
K.
L. NIL.
M. NIL.
N. (1) N/A.
N. (2) N/A.

Me110 Destroyed G. 9/10

GENERAL REPORT.

In formation with 41 Squadron we were ordered to patrol north of base 20,000 feet. After flying for a while, we saw formation of Ju.88 and Me.110. The Squadron then went into line astern, we made an attack, the second attack, I fired two short bursts into the starboard engine of a Me110. This started to smoke, it went down in a steep dive to Port. I followed it down to 10,000 ft firing at the fusalage, the machine gunner stopped firing, then continuing my dive, I fired at the port engine, which was then on fire. I left it at 5,000 feet still in a vertical dive, with both engines on fire.

E. S. Lock.

Signed. E.S. Lock. P/O.

EB G
P7350

G

‘I fired at him and he exploded in mid-air’

‘I was Red 2 of 41 Squadron, flying in formation with the rest of the squadron, when we intercepted a formation of enemy aircraft. We attacked the bombers first… It then developed into a dogfight. I engaged an enemy He 111, which I followed down until it crashed into the river. I climbed back to 8,000ft and saw another enemy He 111, which had left the main formation. I engaged and set his starboard engine on fire. I closed in to about 75 yards and fired two long bursts and smoke came from the fuselage. The enemy aircraft then put his wheels down and started to glide. I stopped firing and followed him down. I was then attacked by a Me 109 [sic] who fired at me from below and wounded me in the leg. As he banked away he stall turned. I fired at him and he exploded in mid-air. I then followed the bomber down until it ditched on the sea about 10 miles from the first one in the mouth of the river. I circled round a boat, which was at hand… I saw the boat go to the enemy aircraft. I was then joined by Red 3. On our return we saw the first bomber which was still floating.’

Flight Lieutenant Eric Lock DSO DFC and Bar

'I wrote myself off'

'On 1st September 1939 I wrote myself off. I thought you've got no chance of lasting through whatever it's going to be.'

Flying Officer Ken Wilkinson (No 19 Squadron)

Ken Wilkinson

Ken Wilkinson was born on 29 June 1918 at Barrow-in-Furness. He joined the RAFVR in March 1939. With his flying training completed and after converting to Spitfires, he joined No 616 Squadron at Kirton-in-Lindsey on 1 October 1940, as a sergeant pilot, moving to No 19 Squadron at Fowlmere on 17 October. He was posted away to 56 OTU Sutton Bridge on 27 January 1941 as an instructor. On 23 October, he joined 1488 Flight at Shoreham. He was sent on a course to Central Gunnery School at Sutton Bridge on 10 May 1942, to become a pilot gunnery instructor, after which he was posted to 11 Group Practice Camp at Martlesham Heath. A further instructional tour of duty with 61 OTU at Rednal followed before, after a refresher course on Spitfires, he joined No 234 Squadron at Skeabrae, Orkney, in April 1943, and then moved to No 165 Squadron at Ibsley on 8 July. From December 1943, he saw the war out as an instructor. Wilkinson was released from the RAF in November 1945. He became a Quantity Surveyor in civilian life and lives in the same house he bought with his wife in 1951.

Left: Armourers loading up a No 19 Squadron Spitfire.

Right: P7350 displaying the No 19 Squadron QV-E code letters of Ken Wilkinson.

P7350
E
QV

'I never saw the aeroplane that shot me down…'

'We were reforming… we'd been in action…. I hadn't fired at anything. The CO said, "15,000 feet over Hornchurch", so there were six of us, but in a ragged formation because we were reforming. I never saw the aeroplane that shot me down… I wasn't looking for it after it hit me either, that would have been stupid.

'The engine was still going, but I must have taken a bullet through the radiator because I could taste the glycol coming through into the cockpit. Also I had no roll control at all; the ailerons were up on both wings. I thought, "I'm not turning"… I just went straight because I knew that once I was in turn if you haven't got any ailerons you can't get out of it… so I glided straight. The first thing you do when you're hit is pull the hood back and then I could taste this glycol even through the oxygen mask… so I just glided, but I was using the engine sometimes, in little spurts. If you're quite high it's bloody cold up there and the engine never got hot because I didn't use it enough. The Spitfire will glide I reckon about two miles per 1,000ft and I was quite high over the southern edge of the Thames Estuary.

'The first thing I did after opening the hood was to look and see where to go. I put the nose down so I could see more in the distance and there was this little yellow square field, recently harvested, near Staplehurst, in Kent, and that's what I aimed for. When I landed, wheels up of course, I slid into an adjacent hop garden. The poles in a hop field are thin bamboo that hold up the vine of the hop. The wings cut through about 30 yards and that stopped me because it's a real forest. You had to be damn careful you didn't emasculate yourself climbing out through it, so I kept my parachute on to get out and to jump off the wing!'

Squadron Leader Basil Gerald 'Stapme' Stapleton DFC, DFC (Dutch)

Basil 'Stapme' Stapleton

Basil Gerald 'Stapme' Stapleton served with No 603 (City of Edinburgh) Squadron AuxAF, flying Spitfires, from December 1939 to March 1941. No 603 Squadron lost 13 pilots during the summer of 1940 with many more seriously injured. 'Stapme's' personal score of six enemy aircraft destroyed, three shared destroyed, eight probably destroyed and two damaged, all achieved on Spitfires during the Battle of Britain, made him one of the outstanding fighter pilots of the period. He was shot down on 7 September 1940 and was awarded the Distinguished Flying Cross on 15 November 1940. 'Stapme' subsequently flew Hurricanes with the Merchant Ship Fighting Unit and as a flight commander on No 257 Squadron, he was an instructor at Central Gunnery School and commanded No 247 Squadron flying Hawker Typhoons in northern France after D-Day. He was awarded the Dutch DFC for his leadership of No 247 Squadron throughout Operation 'Market Garden'. On 23 December 1944 Stapleton became a prisoner of war after he force-landed behind enemy lines when debris from an exploding train that he had attacked punctured the radiator of his Typhoon. 'Stapme' died on 13 April 2010, a month before his 90th birthday.

'You're interfering with the cricket'

'I can hear the controller now, giving us a course to steer for Dungeness… "150 plus"… I looked up and saw this massive gaggle in the distance like a lot of gnats on a summer evening and I thought "where on earth do you start on this lot?" … I can remember thinking "This is serious. These chaps mean business. They're not doing this for fun". The Germans had conquered everything through Europe and now they were bombing our country. I thought, "What are you doing over here? Why? England's a peaceful place; you're interfering with the cricket".'

Squadron Leader Geoffrey Wellum DFC, No 92 (East India) Squadron

Geoffrey Wellum

Geoffrey Wellum was born on 14 August 1921. He joined the RAF on a short service commission in August 1939. When his training was completed in May 1940 he was posted to No 92 (East India) Squadron, where his age and youthful looks earned him the nickname 'Boy'. He was just 19 years old when he first went into combat during the Battle of Britain. On 11 September 1940 he claimed a He 111 destroyed, but his Spitfire, 'QJ-K', was badly shot up in combat with a Bf 109 and had to be sent away for repairs. He was given a new personal Spitfire, coded 'QJ-G', which he flew for the remainder of the Battle. Geoffrey was awarded the DFC in July 1941 and in August was posted to 52 OTU, Aston Down, as an instructor. In March 1942 he became a flight commander with No 65 Squadron at Debden. He was posted to Malta in August 1942, leading eight Spitfires off HMS *Furious* to Luqa. After returning to the UK, he became a test pilot at Gloster Aircraft, testing Hawker Typhoons, and later became a gunnery instructor until the end of the war. Geoffrey was officially credited with a wartime total of three enemy aircraft destroyed, four 'probables' and several damaged. He retired from the RAF in 1961, as a squadron leader, to take up a position with a firm of commodity brokers in the City of London, until his retirement to Cornwall where he still lives. Geoffrey is the author of the highly-acclaimed book 'First Light', which gives a brilliant insight into his experiences in the Battle of Britain.

Left: Geoffrey Wellum (right) and fellow pilot Brian Kingcombe.

Right: and overleaf: Spitfire P7350 with No 92 Squadron's QJ-G code letters, the aircraft of Geoffrey Wellum after 11 September 1940.

QJ
G
P7350

UP
WARNING
FLAPS MUST NOT BE DOWN OR LOWERED AT SPEEDS ABOVE 120 KTS. I.A.S.
ON
WARNING
ISOLATE
PRESS.
REGULATOR MARK XIIA
DELIVERY OXYGEN
FEET SUPPLY AVAILABLE
UP
L R
ON
FUEL
OFF
REMOTE CONTACTOR

G
P7350

'Oh God, this bloke is going to kill me'

'I was shot up badly on three occasions. One time, I had literally to fight my way back to the White Cliffs; on another, there was a German 109 hanging on my tail, who wouldn't let me go. When I saw him, I felt fear, real stark fear. Not "Ooh, this is frightening", but "Oh God, this bloke is going to kill me". Then I got cross. I thought "To hell with this, I'm not ready to go yet". I'll never know how I got away with it. The worst bit was waiting for that phone to go in dispersal. I was more afraid, apprehensive, scared, or whatever you want to call it, waiting at dispersal for that phone to ring. That's when it got to me… but once in the aeroplane, then you were reconciled. You were partners with your aeroplane and you had a job to do.'

Squadron Leader Geoffrey Wellum DFC,
No 92 (East India) Squadron

Peterjohn I
F
SH
3910

SPITFIRE Mk Vb AB910

Spitfire AB910 was one of the initial batch of 500 Mk Vb Spitfires ordered from the Castle Bromwich factory. Fitted with two 20mm cannons and four 0.303in Browning machine guns, and a Rolls-Royce Merlin 45 engine, it was delivered to its first operational unit, No 222 (Natal) Squadron at North Weald, on 22 August 1941. Unfortunately, within days of its arrival the aircraft was damaged during a forced landing at Lympne. After repair, AB910 was re-allocated to No 130 Squadron at Perranporth, Cornwall, to fly convoy protection patrols and fighter escort to daylight bombing raids.

In June 1942 AB910 was delivered to No 133 (Eagle) Squadron at Biggin Hill. It flew 29 operational sorties with this unit, including four on 19 August 1942 during the fierce aerial battles in support of the Dieppe Raid. One of AB910's pilots that day, American Flt Sgt 'Dixie' Alexander, was credited with destroying a Dornier Do 217 bomber whilst flying this Spitfire during these combats.

AB910 continued to fly operationally up to July 1944, serving with No 242 Squadron and then with Nos 416 and 402 (RCAF) Squadrons. With the latter, the aircraft flew numerous cover patrols over the Normandy invasion beach-heads on D-Day, 6 June 1944, and the days following. In almost three years of front-line duties during World War 2, AB910 flew a remarkable total of 143 operational missions; it was damaged on four separate occasions in landing or taxying incidents during the war.

On 13 July 1944, this remarkable Spitfire's long operational flying 'career' came to an end and it was transferred to No 53 Operational Training Unit at Hibaldstow, where it served to the end of the war. Whilst at Hibaldstow AB910 famously flew with a girl on the tail by mistake! On 14 February 1945 LACW Margaret Horton, a WAAF aircraft mechanic, sat on the tail of the aircraft as it taxied out to the take-off point (standard practice in windy weather). The pilot, Flt Lt Neill Cox DFC and Bar, did not know she was there and took off with Margaret still on the aircraft. The combination of her weight on the tail and her grip on the elevator very nearly had disastrous results, but fortunately the pilot was able to maintain control and one circuit later he landed with Margaret still wrapped around the fin!

After the war AB910 served for a year as a radar calibration 'target' aircraft with No 527 Squadron and then with the Radio Warfare Establishment. In 1947 the Spitfire was purchased by Gp Capt Allen Wheeler and flown privately as an air racer for six years, registered as G-AISU and fitted with a four-bladed propeller. During this period AB910 was damaged twice more in ground incidents.

Left: Spitfire VB AB910 in the markings of BM327/SH-F of Flt Lt Tony Cooper in 1944.

Below: Before being donated to the BBMF, AB910 was owned by Vickers-Armstrong.

THROTTLE
MIXTURE
RICH
WEAK
OXYGEN
SUPPLY AVAILABLE
FLAPS MUST NOT BE
DOWN OR LOWERED
AT SPEEDS ABOVE
120 KTS. I.A.S.
GEN
WARNING
START
ISOLATE
FUEL
PRESS.
VOLTS
D.C.
R.P.M.
UP
ALT
REMOTE CONTACTOR
ON
OUT
CONTROL
IS
SET TO
KEEP
LEVER IN
LOWER
GATE ON
GROUND
BEFORE
USING
SET
DOWN
DANGER
LOCK
PORT
RUDDER
BIAS
STBD
RADIATOR
FLAP

In 1953 AB910 was purchased by Vickers-Armstrong Ltd. After being fully refurbished, AB910 was displayed regularly by the renowned Spitfire test pilot Jeffrey Quill and other Vickers test pilots until the company donated the aircraft to the BBMF in 1965. Jeffrey Quill delivered AB910 personally to the Flight at RAF Coltishall, his last ever flight in a Spitfire.

In service with the BBMF, AB910 has suffered damage in four flying-related accidents or incidents. Undercarriage failures in 1972 and 1976 resulted in the Spitfire tipping up on its nose. A ground collision with a Harvard aircraft at Bex, Switzerland, in 1978, was the aircraft's most serious accident. During the take-off roll, the Spitfire hit the taxying Harvard, which had encroached onto the runway heading the opposite way. The Harvard was pushed back a considerable distance with the two aircraft locked together. Fortunately, there was no fire and no serious injuries, but AB910 sustained serious damage. It was subsequently repaired, under an informal arrangement, by a team from the Repair and Salvage Squadron at the RAF Maintenance Unit at Abingdon, eventually re-joining the BBMF three years later. In 2004, an inner tube failure and flat tyre resulted in the aircraft tipping up on its nose on landing at Coningsby. (BBMF Spitfires are now fitted with tubeless wheels and tyres to reduce the chances of similar occurrences).

During a major refurbishment conducted over two and a half years from October 2012, AB910 was stripped down to the barest level and re-built to an 'as new' standard with much improved authenticity including a three-bladed propeller. Today, AB910 is one of only six airworthy Mk V Spitfires worldwide.

Left: The cockpit of AB910.

Right: BBMF Spitfire Mk Vb in the colours of Polish ace Jan Zumbach.

Jan Zumbach

Jan Zumbach was born in Poland but held Swiss citizenship. He joined the Polish Air Force in 1936. After the Germans invaded Poland he escaped, via Rumania, to France where he flew fighters with the French Air Force. Then when France was overrun he escaped to England in June 1940. On 2 August 1940, having been accepted into the RAF, he became a founding member of No 303 (Kosciuszko) Squadron, the unit with which he achieved all but one of his wartime victories. He flew Hurricanes with No 303 Squadron from Northolt during the remainder of the Battle of Britain, claiming eight kills. In January 1941 the squadron re-equipped with Spitfires and Jan Zumbach continued to fly with the unit on fighter sweeps, bomber escorts and 'circuses' over Europe. After a short spell instructing at the start of 1942, he returned to No 303 Squadron in March 1942 as a flight commander. Two months later he was promoted to squadron leader and appointed to command the unit, a duty he performed from May until December 1942. After various staff tours he returned to flying duties in command of No 133 Polish Air Wing, flying P-51 Mustangs. His total wartime score was 13 enemy aircraft confirmed destroyed, plus five 'probables'. After the war he settled in France and continued to lead an exciting and maverick life, reportedly smuggling contraband (especially diamonds) around southern Europe and the Middle East in Dakotas, and flying B-26 Invaders as a mercenary pilot for Biafra. He was found dead in his flat in Paris, in mysterious circumstances, in 1986.

'We developed a highly effective technique of close escort'

'We developed a highly effective technique of close escort. We practically glued ourselves to our charges, a pair of us flanking each bomber and shielding it from attack, at the risk of being shot down ourselves… By making ourselves expendable, we were allowing the other fighter squadrons a free hand to deal with the enemy.'

Wing Commander Jan Zumbach (Poland) Virtuti Militari, Polish Cross of Valour and 3 Bars, DFC and Bar

Right: Flt Lt Jan Zumbach alongside his Spitfire Mk V BM144 RF-D, together with Wg Cdr Stefan Witorzenc (centre) and Flt Lt Zygmunt Bienkowski.

Don Kingaby

Don Kingaby joined the RAF in 1939 and flew Spitfires during the Battle of Britain as a sergeant pilot with Nos 266 and 92 Squadrons, claiming five enemy aircraft destroyed and three damaged. In November 1940 he shot down six Bf 109s, three of them (plus a 'probable') in a single day. During the offensive fighter sweeps of 1941 he claimed another 12 enemy aircraft destroyed, being dubbed by the press the '109 specialist'. He was awarded the DFM three times (the only RAF pilot of World War 2 to receive two bars to the DFM), before being commissioned in November 1941. With only a couple of brief rest periods, Don Kingaby flew Spitfires operationally up to July 1944, as a squadron pilot, flight commander, squadron commander and Wing leader. He flew some 300 operational sorties and scored a total of 21 victories against enemy aircraft, as well as two shared kills, six probable kills and 10 damaged, the majority of his kills were against Bf 109s. He finished the war on the staff of the Advanced Gunnery School and afterwards remained in the RAF until 1958. Don Kingaby subsequently moved to the United States, where he resided until his death on New Year's Eve 1990, aged 70.

'Bits flew off him, there was a great cloud of smoke and he went straight in'

'We were fighting just above the sea and when I began to throw him off my tail, he climbed above me and tried to half roll down onto me again. At the last moment he realised that he was too low down to do this and, to avoid going straight into the drink, he had to roll out again in the same direction as myself. I saw this happening and yanked the throttle back to slow down as quickly as possible. The 109 came out about 150 yards ahead of me and I let him have it from dead astern. Bits flew off him, there was a great cloud of smoke and he went straight in.'

Wing Commander Don Kingaby DSO, AFC, DFM and two Bars, DFC (USA), Belgian Croix de Guerre

'The theory of a fight between fighter planes is very simple'

'The theory of a fight between fighter planes is very simple. You see the enemy, grab for his coat-tails, hold on to them, put your guns up against his back pocket and press the trigger. But while you are reaching for his coat-tails, he is reaching for yours. You make your grab and he twirls out of the way and into position to make his grab. Whereupon you twirl with a twist that will put you in a fair way to grab him and so on and so on, grab - twirl - twist, grab - twirl - twist, sometimes for quite a long time… until at last somebody has grabbed hold for good and the other fellow starts to die.'

Major Don Gentile DFC, No 133 (Eagle) Squadron RAF and later USAAF

Don Gentile

Don Gentile actually flew BBMF Spitfire Mk Vb AB910 twice when they were both on the strength of No 133 (Eagle) Squadron in 1942. Don was an American citizen from Ohio, the son of Italian immigrants, who joined the Royal Canadian Air Force in July 1941, before the USA was drawn into World War 2. He served with No 133 Squadron flying Spitfires from February 1942 and his first kills, against a Junkers Ju 88 and a Focke-Wulf Fw 190, were made on 19 August 1942 during Operation 'Jubilee'. Transferring to the USAAF in September 1942, he flew P-47 Thunderbolts and P-51 Mustangs with the 336th Fighter Squadron, 4th Fighter Group, of the 8th Air Force. He became one of the highest-scoring American fighter aces of the war, credited with 19 aerial victories, three damaged and six ground kills, in 350 combat hours flown, in addition to the two victories he claimed while flying with the RAF. After the war Don Gentile remained in the air force. Sadly, he was killed flying a T-33 Shooting Star jet trainer on 28 January 1951.

Left: Don Gentile flew AB910 during his time with the American Eagle Squadrons. This rare colour photograph taken after he was transferred to the 336th Fighter Squadron of the USAAF, shows him alongside his P-51B Shangri-La*, together with fellow pilot John Godfrey.*

NZ Y

Dixie' Alexander

ichard 'Dixie' Alexander was an American citizen rom Illinois who joined the Royal Canadian Air Force n October 1940, before the USA was drawn into World War 2. He subsequently found himself serving, rom February 1942, with one of the RAF's 'Eagle' quadrons. 'Dixie' was a flight sergeant with No 133 Eagle) Squadron when he flew Spitfire Mk Vb AB910 n one of the aircraft's sorties during the Dieppe aid (Operation 'Jubilee') on 19 August 1942, claiming kill against a Do 217 – the aircraft's only kill. The Eagle' squadrons were manned by mainly American ilots, with British groundcrew. In September 1942, Dixie' transferred to the USAAF and flew Spitfires nd P-51s in the Mediterranean area until he was hot down over Italy and became a prisoner of war n 30 May 1944. His final tally was six confirmed kills. ost war he remained in the USAAF until an accident n Germany in 1947 resulted in the amputation of is right arm and he was medically discharged. He eturned to the USA to live in Illinois and finally etired from working after the loss of a leg in 1980. Dixie' Alexander died in 1993, aged 79.

eft: Spitfire Mk Vb BM635 WZ-Y of the 309th Fighter quadron, 31st Fighter Group, 8th Air Force.

'I singled out one "217" and closed to about 300 yards'

'I saw six Do 217s just as they were dropping their bombs on a convoy. I singled out one "217" and closed to about 300 yards. I fired bursts into him until my cannons were exhausted. There was good return fire at the beginning, but I believe I must have killed the gunner who was giving me trouble. I had observed numerous hits on the enemy aircraft and his port engine was smoking. By this time we were south of Dieppe and over land, and I continued to fire short bursts of '303' into him and he made a gentle turn, dropped down and crash landed in a field some two or three miles south of the town. I did a tight turn, came back and fired one burst at the aircraft and crew as they were scrambling for cover, and then returned to Lympne alone.'

Captain Richard L. 'Dixie' Alexander, No 133 (Eagle) Squadron RAF and later USAAF, flying AB910

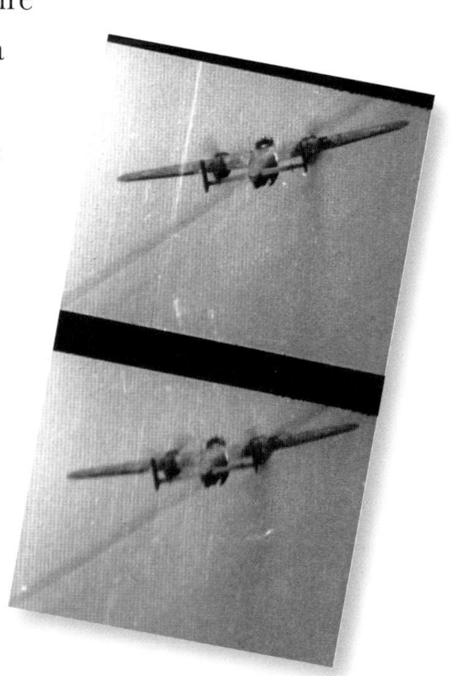

Lineshoot for home – To show how the dear boy earns his money!

Tony Cooper

Tony Cooper spent his first three years of the war with the RAF as a flying instructor, mostly in Canada, but continually requested to be posted to an operational fighter squadron. His wish was eventually granted in 1943 and after training on Spitfires he joined No 64 Squadron in July that year. From then on he was involved in numerous operations over Europe: fighter sweeps, bomber escort missions, shipping strikes and also ground attack sorties. By D-Day, Tony was a flight commander on the squadron, which he frequently led in the air. During the month of June 1944, across D-Day, he flew 75 hours. He remained flying with No 64 Squadron, converting to Mk IX Spitfires, until November 1944, by which time he had flown some 160 operational sorties. He had also survived five forced landings, two of them at night, two on fire and one as a result of being hit by enemy fire. He was posted to be an instructor at the Spitfire OTU at Hibaldstow, where he once actually flew Spitfire AB910 and witnessed the famous 'girl on the tail' incident from the ground. When the war was over Tony Cooper returned to the family business in Suffolk. He passed away on 26 January 2017, 11 days before his 101st birthday. BBMF personnel formed the pall bearer party and carried his coffin at his funeral.

Above and left: AB910 in the D-Day colours of Tony Cooper's SH-F.

Overleaf: Tony Cooper's logbook for 6 June 1944, D-Day.

- JUNE 6th 1944 - THE ALLIED INVASION OF FRANCE -

JUNE	6	SPITFIRE VB	SHF	SELF	SOLO	FIGHTER COVER FOR UTAH BEACH -
"	6	SPITFIRE VB	SHF	SELF	SOLO	FIGHTER COVER FOR OMAHA BEACH -
"	7	SPITFIRE VB	SHF	SELF	SOLO	FIGHTER COVER FOR UTAH BEACH -
"	7	SPITFIRE VB	SHF	SELF	SOLO	FIGHTER COVER FOR UTAH BEACH -
"	7	SPITFIRE VB	SHK	SELF	SOLO	FIGHTER COVER FOR OMAHA BEACH -
"	8	SPITFIRE VB	SHC	SELF	SOLO	FIGHTER COVER FOR OMAHA BEACH

103.50	198.50	5.00	179.05	.15	.30 7.30 29.05 35.00
	1.40		1.00		Patrolling at 0520 hrs. - Navy shelling coast defenses - First landing made at 0620 hrs. - Nearly shot down by Thunderbolt - Spitfire in front actually was - Another Spit hit by naval shell + blew up - General Brock's "benefit"!
			2.05		Hun bombers attacked 'invasion fleet' - Tremendous return fire from ships - one bomber destroyed -
	2.00		.20		Beachheads established - Another airborne division (Gliders) dropped in successfully -
	2.30				Landings continuing - Naval units bombard inland targets - (Nelson Warspite etc).
			2.35		Very bad visibility - No attacks - Sent 40 miles out to sea on return owing to reciprocal homing vectors - Very shaky experience - Brought in eventually by rockets -
	2.20				No Huns - Hun tanks shelling destroyers!

LOCATION FOR WING TIP
STEADYING TRESTLE
LOCATION FOR WING TIP
STEADYING TRESTLE

'Our original feeling of pent-up excitement now turned to one of total awe'

'Opening up into "battle" formation, we reached a few miles off the French coast at 05.20hrs and, as the dawn broke, we were able to survey our patrol area. Our original feeling of pent-up excitement now turned to one of total awe at the incredible scene that presented itself. The coast and most of the beaches were almost hidden by a pall of dust and smoke left from the previous evening's huge softening up bombing raids and the naval bombardment, but below us and as far as the eye could see was a multitude of ships, thousands upon thousands, formed into one gigantic armada, all heading to the beaches to disembark their cargos of Allied troops and equipment.

'That day the squadron carried out four patrols, including one at last light, and this was to become the norm for the next few weeks. Pilots sometimes had to return home at night, often in the most unpleasant weather conditions. Formating only on the blue exhaust flames from their companion aircraft (the navigation lights were kept switched off), they had to find their way back to base, dodging the barrage balloons that protected the blacked-out English coastal towns and then land by thc dim light of goose-neck flares at their tiny advanced landing grounds.'

Flight Lieutenant Tony Cooper Legion d'Honneur, No 64 Squadron Spitfire Mk Vb on D-Day

KWICHERBICHEN
UK
ZA947

C-47 DAKOTA III ZA947

C-47 Dakota III ZA947 is the last of its type serving with the Royal Air Force, which once operated over 1,900 'Daks'. This Dakota was constructed as a C-47A by Douglas at Long Beach, California, USA, in 1942. It was delivered to the USAAF with the serial number 42-24338 on 7 September 1943. A little over a week later, on 16 September, it was transferred to the Royal Canadian Air Force (RCAF) and re-designated as a Dakota III. The Canadians allocated this particular Dakota the RCAF serial number '661'.

During World War 2, Dakota '661' served entirely in Canada. Little is known about the aircraft's specific duties, although it is thought that the aircraft was with No 164 Squadron, one of the RCAF's premier transport squadrons based at Moncton, New Brunswick. From Moncton, No 164 Squadron's work involved moving passengers and freight around Newfoundland, particularly to Goose Bay and Gander.

After World War 2 had ended, Dakota '661' operated in support of the Canadian forces in Europe from 1965 until 1969, when the aircraft was declared surplus to requirements with the RCAF and sold to Scottish Aviation at Prestwick, which was operating on behalf of the Royal Aircraft Establishment (RAE). As the Canadian serial '661' did not comply with standard RAF serials, it was given the RAF designation KG661.

For some years KG661 was based with the RAE at West Freugh, a coastal airfield in Wigtownshire, near Portpatrick, five miles south-east of Stranraer in Dumfries and Galloway, Scotland. From West Freugh the aircraft was used in various RAE trials over the Luce Bay ranges, particularly dropping experimental sonobuoys into the sea and launching remotely-piloted vehicles. Whilst based at West Freugh, the aircraft was given the name *Portpatrick Princess*.

In the late1970s it was realised that the serial number KG661 had, in fact, previously been allocated to another Dakota which had crashed and been written off. The error was reported and in July 1979 the Dakota was allocated the 'modern' serial ZA947, which explains why the serial worn by the BBMF Dakota does not match the age or era of the aircraft.

In its later years of service with the RAE, ZA947 was based at Farnborough. It was also fitted with a stronger floor and 'modern' airline-style seats from a DH Comet.

In 1990, ZA947 was involved in an accident at Farnborough when the navigator accidentally retracted the landing gear on the ground whilst the engines were running. As the undercarriage collapsed the port propeller hit the ground, destroying the reduction gear box, debris smashed into the fuselage and the aircraft's port wing was also damaged beyond repair.

The contract to repair and carry out an overhaul of the aircraft was awarded to Air Atlantique. A port wing was obtained from a derelict Dakota in Malta and brought to the UK. It was badly corroded and the company re-skinned much of it and replaced several ribs and other components of its internal structure. The refurbished wing was then taken to Farnborough and fitted to ZA947, together with a new engine and propeller. Once it was flyable, the aircraft was ferried to Coventry for a complete overhaul.

When the Defence Research Agency – the successor to the RAE – declared ZA947 surplus to their requirements and offered it up for disposal in 1992, the aircraft was adopted by RAF Strike Command to be issued to the BBMF. It was taken on charge by the Flight in March 1993.

The Dakota was, perhaps, originally intended by those in command to be a support and training aircraft for the BBMF, replacing the Flight's DH Devon C1, which was auctioned off in 1998. As there are now no other multi-engine tail-wheel aircraft in RAF service outside the BBMF, the Dakota is indeed an important training asset used for initial training of aircrew for the BBMF multi-engine aircraft and for renewing the currency of the Flight's 'bomber' pilots each year. However, the Dakota is also a sought-after display aircraft in its own right, appearing regularly on the air show circuit and at commemorative events.

Left: BBMF C-47 Dakota ZA947 in No 233 Squadron colours.

'Bandits! … There's hunderts of the buggers'

'I took part in the Arnhem drop with 233 Squadron. For the launch I had a fully laden glider in tow… Four days after the launch we were asked for a maximum effort to replenish the main force, now contained within a small perimeter around the Waal Bridge. I carried 16 350lb panniers of petrol and ammunition. The dispatchers, soldiers of the Royal Army Service Corps [RASC] as it was then, did a wonderful job in a single run over the dropping zone. That was a relief because the anti-aircraft fire was the thickest I had ever seen and the Dakota casualties were high … As we sped away our regular dispatcher, an Irish RASC private, shouted from the astrodome which was the sole way of seeing behind, "Bandits!", the code for attacking fighters. We had taught him the standard way of reporting their whereabouts, such as "port, starboard beam, quarter, ahead, astern, high or low." Nothing but silence followed his initial shout. The awful gap seemed so long and worrying that I asked, "Come on, Paddy, where are they?" After a further aeon of seconds came the answer, "There's hunderts of the buggers." By then I was corkscrewing close to the ground, making the fighters' task nearly impossible and once again we were spared anything but a few bullet holes.'

Air Commodore Alastair Mackie CBE DFC and Bar, No 233 Squadron

Alastair Mackie

Alastair Mackie was commissioned as a pilot officer in May 1941. He began his operational flying in Wellington bombers over the North African desert and later converted to the Consolidated B-24 Liberator with No 178 Squadron, earning his first DFC in April 1943. Returning to the UK he flew C-47 Dakotas with No 233 Squadron and took part in the D-Day operations, dropping paratroopers and supplies. After D-Day he flew military supplies into forward airfields on the continent and brought casualties back to the UK. He also took part in the Arnhem battle, towing a glider and subsequently re-supplying the cut-off paratroopers from the air. He was awarded a bar to his DFC in December 1944. After the war Mackie remained in the RAF on a permanent commission. He served on the staff of the Central Flying School teaching future instructors in a variety of aircraft from Tiger Moths to Lancasters. On promotion to wing commander he flew Canberra bombers at RAF Waddington and then commanded one of the first Avro Vulcan squadrons. He eventually retired from the RAF in September 1968 as an air commodore with a CBE to add to his two DFCs. He pursued a career in law and became a leading light in the campaign for nuclear disarmament.

Right: Dakotas overfly a drop zone during D-Day operations.

ZA947

Colin Lynch

Colin Lynch was born and brought up in the British Raj. He joined the RAF in December 1940 and was selected and trained as an RAF observer. He joined No 31 Squadron at Agartala in Assam, India, in May 1943, aged 20, as a sergeant navigator on C-47 Dakotas, flying air drop sorties and supplying the troops of the Fourteenth Army in Burma. He was wounded by Japanese shrapnel whilst flying supplies into Myitkyina in mid-1944 in support of the Chindits, but quickly returned to flying duties. By March 1945 he had flown over 2,000 operational hours (two tours) and 326 sorties and reached the rank of warrant officer. He finished the war working in the Air Booking Centre in New Delhi and living in the family home there. He elected to be 'demobbed' in England rather than stay in India and settled in London, working as a graphic designer until he retired.

Left: BBMF Dakota in the livery of No 267 'Pegasus' Squadron that operated in the Mediterranean and Burma.

'Bursts of gunfire shot past on both sides…'

'We were on an early morning mission to drop ammunition para-packs at the drop zone [DZ] at Tiddim. We got there without trouble, reduced height, checked the ground signal by the DZ, and went into the circuit at 300ft. Another Dakota was there already, with Scottish Flight Sergeant Richards – from my 'basha' – flying it. My pilot, Flying Officer Larsen, was lining us up behind Richards to approach the DZ, when there was a rattle of anti-aircraft fire from the ground. At the same time, through the windscreen, we could see three Jap dive bombers, escorted by four Oscar fighters, attacking the DZ. Before we could blink, three of the fighters peeled away, and opened fire on our Daks from behind. Bursts of gunfire shot past on both sides, but not one hit us! But Richards was hit; his aircraft burst into flames and veered out of control across the valley. We banked hard right and swooped down low over the river to try to lose the fighters. As we did so, we saw the other Dak hit the cliff across the far bank and blow up.'

Warrant Officer Colin Lynch, navigator, No 31 Squadron

'...we received several hits from an Oerlikon gun'

'We were part of a re-supply operation to Arnhem on 21 September 1944, with a load of oil and mortar bombs in 16 panniers. We had four Army men [Royal Army Service Corps dispatchers] aboard to put the load out when we reached the dropping zone [DZ], so there were eight men aboard, including Flying Officer Mike Ades [pilot and captain], Flight Sergeant Ken Dorville [co-pilot], myself [navigator], and Flight Sergeant Jack Hickey AFM [wireless operator]. Everything went OK until we reached the DZ, where we had to run through a lot of light 'flak'. I think we were hit, but not seriously, and we began the return trip. About 10 minutes after leaving Arnhem, at 5,000ft, we received several hits from an Oerlikon gun on the ground, being hit in the port wing and in the fuselage, one shot came through the floor just in front of Mike's feet, and out through the top of the cabin.

'Several minutes later, the Army men drew attention to flames coming through the floor, and after telling Mike, I tried to put them out with the fire extinguisher, but they had a firm hold by that time and I had to abandon the extinguisher. Mike decided to try to reach the British lines before crash landing, and when we were down to 2,000ft told me to get the Army chaps into crash-landing positions. Before going aft to do so, I clipped my parachute pack onto my harness. I went back to the aft door, where Jack was standing, reassuring the Army men and telling them we were going to crash-land. They shouted that it was too late, and pointed over my shoulder. I turned, and saw that in the last few seconds the forward part of the fuselage had been enveloped in flame and smoke. Jack and I decided the time had come to abandon the aircraft, and told the Army men to jump with us. I went out, and Jack followed... Years later I discovered that the Army men also jumped; they all became P.O.W.s. The pilots were trapped by the flames, and died of burns. By the time we jumped, we were only at about 800ft and so it only took us about 20 seconds to reach the ground.'

Flying Officer Fred Dyer (RAAF), navigator No 233 Squadron

Fred Dyer

Fred Dyer came from Adelaide and enlisted in the Royal Australian Air Force (RAAF) on 18 July 1942, as a navigator. He trained in Australia and Canada. In November 1943 he was posted to England and, after further training, he was assigned to No 233 Squadron in late June 1944, with the rank of pilot officer. Based at Blakehill Farm, Wiltshire, No 233 Squadron operated C-47 Dakotas with RAF Transport Command. Fred Dyer was one of a number of replacements for aircrew that had become casualties during the D-Day operations. The squadron became a specialist casualty evacuation 'air ambulance' unit, before being involved in the Battle of Arnhem in September 1944. After being shot down and baling out on 21 September during an Arnhem re-supply flight, Dyer and wireless operator Jack Hickey both landed unhurt, 50 yards apart, in a small clearing in a large forest. They ran off in a westerly direction, away from enemy rifle fire; a couple of rounds actually hitting the trees around them. Subsequently Dyer and Hickey evaded capture with the help of local Dutch people and were handed over to the advancing Allied forces on 2 October 1944. After the war Fred Dyer returned to his native Australia. He died on 26 July 1998, a week before his 77th birthday.

Left: Cockpit of the BBMF Dakota.

V

Marjorie Clark

Marjorie Clark (nee Wright) joined the WAAF in August 1941, aged 18, initially as an 'aircraft-hand/ tailoress'. In 1943 she volunteered for air ambulance duties and underwent training as a nursing orderly, after which she joined No 233 Squadron at Blakehill Farm. Later she served with the other Dakota squadrons involved in casualty evacuation at both Down Ampney and Broadwell. Between December 1944 and the end of the war in Europe in May 1945, Marjorie flew over 260 hours in Dakotas and personally evacuated 420 stretcher cases and 148 walking or sitting wounded. The BBMF provided her with a personal flypast in 2015 in recognition of what she had done during the war. Marjorie was one of the last surviving 'Flying Nightingales' when she passed away in December 2016, aged 93.

Left: RAF Dakota IIIs of No 46 Group at B2-Bazenville, on the Normandy coast, loading casualties for evacuation to England.

'What do I remember most? The smell, the good humour, the courage…'

'I trained as a nursing orderly for the Air Ambulance Service at Hendon and I served at all three stations involved in the air ambulance operations: Blakehill Farm, Down Ampney and Broadwell. We flew mail and military equipment into France, Belgium, Holland and Germany and brought casualties back on the return journey, usually 18 stretcher cases and six walking wounded. We did not expect any special recognition for doing a responsible job that we felt privileged to do, and the opportunity to fly was so exciting that only an idiot would have turned it down. What do I remember most? The smell, the good humour, the courage, the professional footballer who had both legs amputated, the soldier who had been run over by a tank track (I accompanied him to Radcliffe Infirmary) and many other things. We got one shilling a day Air Crew pay (a lot of money in those days), an egg for breakfast and flying boots and gloves, and close touch with those really concerned with the war effort. It was very satisfying and rewarding.'

Leading Aircraft Woman Marjorie Clark, nursing orderly No 233 Squadron

Peter Bailey

George 'Peter' Bailey joined the RAF in January 1941, aged 18, to train as a pilot. He received his 'wings' in Canada in April 1942 and stayed on for a year as an instructor. He was then sent home to the UK and flew Vickers Wellingtons to gain experience of twin-engine heavy aircraft, before joining RAF Transport Command and converting to the C-47 Dakota. With No 233 Squadron he flew Dakotas on the D-Day operations, the re-supply and casualty evacuation sorties afterwards, and over Arnhem. He was awarded an American DFC for his achievements over Normandy and Arnhem. He then transferred to No 243 Squadron in the Pacific area, flying a brand new Dakota from America to Australia and then working in New Guinea, Borneo and the Philippines. After the war he remained in the RAF and took part in the Berlin Airlift in 1948-49, flying a Dakota to Berlin and back 250 times. After an exchange tour with the RAAF as a flight commander on a Dakota unit, he commanded No 89 Squadron flying photo-reconnaissance twin-jet English Electric Canberras in Germany. As a wing commander he became OC the VIP Squadron at Northolt and flew many VIPs and members of the Royal Family around the world. He finally retired from the RAF in 1970; he lived and worked in South Africa for eight years and then returned to the UK for another eight years, before eventually retiring to Australia in 1986.

'The job we were doing was so dangerous that they issued us all with American flak suits'

'I was a pilot on No 233 Squadron and towed gliders on the D-Day operations. On the night of 5/6 June 1944, I took off from Blakehill Farm at 22:50 towing a Horsa glider to Drop Zone 'K', near Caen. The glider was loaded with Royal Engineers tasked with blowing up certain bridges at Troarn, east of Caen. Ours was the second of five gliders to be released. We didn't have fighter protection because it took place at night, and we didn't have any armament at all. The job we were doing was so dangerous that they issued us all with American flak suits, but they were cumbersome and uncomfortable to wear. So I used to fold mine up and sit on it because I figured that if anything was going to get me, it would be coming from underneath. We were shot at from the ground on the way in and on the way out. Over the Channel we could see an armada of ships. As we approached the coast of Normandy I talked to the pilots of the glider I was towing over the intercom… I wished them luck and released them at about 2,500ft. Then we had to get back… We returned the following night to deliver supplies, mostly ammunition. We carried two soldiers whose job it was to dispatch the cargo with a parachute to break its fall. This time we didn't have the advantage of surprise, so we were shot at and badly damaged, but, happily, we didn't catch fire.'

Wing Commander Peter Bailey, No 233 Squadron

UK
UK

JX B
LF363
DO NOT FORGET
TO CHECK
PULL DOWN STEP

HURRICANE Mk IIC LF363

Hurricane LF363 was built at the Hawker Aircraft factory at Langley, near Slough in Berkshire, during the winter of 1943, as a Mk IIC fitted with four 20mm cannons and a Rolls-Royce Merlin XX engine. It was first flown on New Year's Day 1944 and was delivered to the RAF, initially to No 5 Maintenance Unit (MU) at Kemble, on 28 January.

On 30 March an ATA ferry pilot collected LF363 from Kemble and delivered it to No 63 Squadron at Turnhouse near Edinburgh. This unit had recently given up its Allison-engined North American Mustang Mk Is, which it had used for Tactical Reconnaissance, and it was now flying Hurricanes to train for naval artillery spotting, in preparation for 'D-Day'.

LF363 was re-allocated to No 309 (Polish) Squadron based at Drem, near North Berwick in East Lothian, Scotland, on 23 May 1944. Like the unit's other Hurricanes, LF363 was fitted with a camera conversion for maritime reconnaissance. The aggressive Polish pilots of No 309 Squadron were deeply disappointed to be moved so far from the action during the D-Day period. However, in October 1944, No 309 Squadron received a full complement of new P-51 Mustang IIIs. They were back in business and the Hurricanes, including LF363, were taken away.

For the remainder of the war LF363 served in non-operational roles with several units. At war's end it was with No 62 Operational Training Unit at Ouston. Subsequently, it was on charge at Middle Wallop and with the Fighter Command Communications Squadron at Northolt. By February 1948 it was with the Station Flight at Thorney Island, apparently in a sorry state, classified as 'u/s awaiting spares'. Following repairs, LF363 took part in the Battle of Britain flypast over London in September 1948, but soon after it suffered a forced landing. It was sent to Hawker's at Langley, where it sat in the open air with no apparent future planned, except probably to be scrapped.

Fortunately, it was saved from that fate, not least by the intervention of the Air Officer Commanding (AOC) of Fighter Command's No 11 Group, AVM Sir Stanley Vincent CB DFC AFC. During the Battle of Britain in 1940 the then Gp Capt Stanley Vincent had been the Station Commander at Northolt whilst Hurricane units were operating from the airfield. Before he retired he wanted to see an RAF Hurricane airworthy again as a commemoration of all that the type had achieved in World War 2. He also harboured a dream of personally leading the annual Battle of Britain flypast over London in a Hurricane. When LF363 was declared fit for flight in the summer of 1949 it was ferried back to Thorney Island, but the pilot could not lower the undercarriage and performed a wheels-up landing on the grass beside the runway. Vincent was determined that the Hurricane would be fit to fly for the Battle of Britain flypast and so, in just six weeks of hard work by the long-suffering groundcrew, it was made airworthy again. Sir Stanley Vincent led the Battle of Britain flypast over London in LF363 on 15 September 1949 as his 'swansong'.

Between 1949 and 1956, LF363 was held and maintained, rather unofficially, by a series of front-line squadrons and Station Flights. It flew on ceremonial occasions such as leading the Battle of Britain flypasts in London each year and also appeared in various films. In July 1957, after a major re-fit at Hawkers, LF363 became a founding aircraft of the RAF Historic Flight, the forerunner of the BBMF, when the Flight was inaugurated at Biggin Hill.

On 11 September 1991, on a flight from Coningsby to Jersey, LF363 suffered a mechanical failure, which resulted in a crash landing at RAF Wittering when the engine failed completely at a late stage of the approach. The aircraft was seriously damaged by the crash and the ensuing fierce fire; fortunately the pilot escaped with a broken ankle and minor burns. LF363 was completely re-built by Historic Flying Ltd between 1994 and 1998 when it flew again for the first time in seven years, subsequently re-joining the BBMF. It now appears as an eight-machine-gun-armed Mk IIA.

Left: Hurricane Mk IIC LF363 in the colours of 'Darkie' Clowes' JX-B.

Left: Four No I Squadron pilots in France inspecting a German machine gun.
Left to right they are: Flg Off Paul Richey, Sqn Ldr P. J. H 'Bull' Halahan (OC), Sgt A.V. 'Darkie' Clowes and Flt Lt P. R. 'Johnny' Walker.

Below and right: 'Darkie' Clowes and his Hurricane P3395, JX-B.

Below right: The Hurricane of 'Darkie' Clowes after its crash landing.

Paul Richey

Paul Richey joined the Hawker Hurricane equipped No I Squadron at Tangmere in March 1939. During the Battle of France Paul Richey claimed 8.5 kills against enemy aircraft, but was forced to bale out twice after being hit by enemy fire. In a fierce aerial combat on 19 May 1940, he had just downed his third Heinkel He 111 in short order, when he was hit by a burst from one of the bomber's rear gunners. He sustained a serious bullet wound to the neck and crash-landed. He was hospitalised until mid-June, but finally made his way home to the UK, where he found that he had been awarded the DFC. After a long period of rehabilitation, during which he wrote his much acclaimed book, 'Fighter Pilot', he returned to flying duties in the spring of 1941 with a posting to No 609 Squadron, with whom he flew 53 fighter sweep missions over enemy territory in Spitfires. After a rest tour as a staff officer he returned to command No 609 Squadron in June 1942, now flying the new Hawker Typhoon. Subsequently he was posted to India as a wing commander and led No 165 and No 189 Wings flying Hurricane Mk IVs, before being invalided home in February 1944. After the war Paul remained in the RAF for a time and commanded No 601 Squadron flying DH Vampire jet fighters. When he retired from the RAF he became an oil company executive. Paul Richey died on 23 February 1989, aged 72.

‘Clowes put up a very good show… ’

‘On 23 November 1939 a Heinkel 111 was brought down near Metz by Blue Section of ‘B’ Flight. It was on fire, losing height rapidly when a bunch of French Moranes came rushing in, all so eager to have a bang that one of them knocked most of Sergeant Clowes’ tail off and the Morane pilot had to bale out. Clowes put up a very good show getting his machine back to the airfield, although he had to land at 120mph to keep control. He overshot and nosed over. I saw him straight after this little effort and, though he was laughing, he was trembling violently and couldn’t talk coherently. I had a good look at his aircraft too. One elevator and half the rudder were completely gone.’

Wing Commander Paul Richey DFC and Bar, No 1 Squadron during the Battle of France and author of ‘Fighter Pilot’ first published 1941

'I was on fire... '

'We were sent up to intercept some bombers. The Me 109s [sic] came down on us and I shot at one of them. I came down to have another go somewhere over Colchester and I was hit by a German cannon shell in the gravity fuel tank just behind the dashboard. It exploded and blew burning petrol into the cockpit. I was on fire. There was only one thing to do and that was to get out as fast as possible. I was badly burned, but I rolled the aircraft over and came down by parachute from 14,000ft. I was conscious all the time. When you are in a situation like that the adrenalin kicks in and you know straight away what needs to be done. Either stay in the aircraft and be dead, or get out and have a chance of staying alive. Simple as that. It was the first time I'd used a parachute. I think I was jolly lucky, in a way. I was picked up by some local people. First a young girl arrived, aged 10 or 12, and she had her younger sister with her. I think I said "hello". Then some men came and took me away by motor car. I wasn't in pain at the time; I was in acute discomfort. The pain comes later. Burns are rather uncomfortable.'

Flight Lieutenant Maurice Mounsdon, No 56 Squadron, 1940

Maurice Mounsdon

Maurice Mounsdon began his flying training in August 1939 and subsequently joined No 56 Squadron at Digby on 3 June 1940. He shared in the destruction of a Dornier Do 17 on 3 July and during the Battle of Britain he claimed two more enemy aircraft destroyed, two probably destroyed and two damaged. On 31 August he was shot down in Hurricane Mk I R4197 'US-C' over Colchester by a Bf 109. He landed by parachute near the village of Great Easter and was picked up, badly burned, by local villagers; a nurse cared for him until he was moved to Black Notley Hospital near Braintree, which at the time specialised in plastic surgery. Maurice spent the next nine months in various hospitals, including the Queen Victoria Hospital, East Grinstead, undergoing pioneering skin grafts and becoming a member of 'The Guinea Pig Club' for burned aircrew. He returned to ground duties in June 1941 on the staff of the Station Headquarters at North Weald. In April 1942 he returned to flying duties as an instructor at No 4 FIS. He served as a flying instructor for the remainder of the war at No 22 EFTS at Cambridge and then No 21 EFTS at Booker. He was released from the RAF in February 1946 as a flight lieutenant and eventually settled in Menorca.

Right: Cockpit of Hurricane Mk IIC, LF363.

ULL RED HANDLE
ORE FLIGHT
GEN FAIL
VHF COMM
START MASTER ENGAGED
BUZZER WARNING WHEELS NOT LOCKED DOWN
WHEELS LOCKED UP GREEN INDICATES WHEELS LOCKED DOWN
PORT LIGHT ON STBD O/L TANK EMPTY
9LB BOOST MAX
BOOST CONTROL CUT-OUT
PRESS TO TEST O/L LIGHTS
EMERGENCY USE ONLY
BOOSTER COIL
PRESSURE HEAD HEAT
NAVIGATION LIGHTS
FUEL GAUGE SELECTOR
MAIN TANKS ON
RESERVE ON
RUDDER BIAS
TAKE-OFF
UP
SELECTOR MUST BE RETURNED TO NEUTRAL AFTER OPERATION
DOWN
PULL
FLIGHT
OVERLOAD FUEL TANKS

OIL
9 GALLS
AIRSPACE
1½ GALLS

Tim Elkington

John 'Tim' Elkington, known as 'Tim', was commissioned on 14 July 1940 and joined No 1 Squadron flying Hurricanes at RAF Northolt. During the Battle of Britain he claimed a Messerschmitt Bf 109 destroyed before he was shot down and wounded in Hurricane P3173 on 16 August 1940. After recovering from his wounds he was posted to No 55 OTU as an instructor and in 1941 joined No 134 Squadron to embark on the aircraft carrier HMS *Argus*, bound for Russia. From there he escorted Russian bombers and trained Russian pilots to fly the Hurricane. During this period he claimed one German Dornier Do 215 shared destroyed, a Junkers Ju 88 probably destroyed and another shared damaged. He returned from Russia in January 1942 and served with the Merchant Ship Fighter Unit until August 1942. After a short period back with No 1 Squadron, he joined No 539 Squadron flying night-fighter Hurricanes. In early 1943, he joined No 197 Squadron and flew the mighty Hawker Typhoon on numerous fighter-bomber operations from RAF Tangmere. Tim was then posted to No 67 Squadron at Alipore, Calcutta, India, to fly Hurricane Mk IICs, before commanding the Air Fighting Development Unit and then the Tactical & Weapon Development Unit in India. He returned home in 1946 and enjoyed a varied post-war career before retiring from the RAF in December 1975.

'Leaving a burning aircraft is easy… '

'I achieved possible success in my first encounter with the enemy on 15 August 1940. A smoking Me 109 [sic] disappearing seawards through the clouds near Harwich. But the next day I became the 18th victim of Helmut Wick when we were intercepting a raid on Tangmere. He was quite an experienced chap, so I'm not too put out! Leaving a burning aircraft is easy. You just throw yourself over the side. But first, make sure that you disconnect your radio and oxygen connections… On the second attempt, I was out. Lovely sunny day – Portsmouth visible through the haze. No pain, just blood. But I was over the sea and had not thought to inflate my Mae West. I remembered nothing more until there was a freckle-faced ambulance girl cutting my trousers off. A strange homecoming! I now know that Sergeant Fred Berry, my Section Leader, came to my rescue and somehow, with slipstream presumably, drifted me onto West Wittering. But only just! Without his aid I would have drowned … Sadly, Fred Berry was killed on 1 September before I was able to thank him.'

Wing Commander John 'Tim' Elkington, No 1 Squadron, 1940

'... I was grateful for the ruggedness of that machine'

'Completing my turn, I came out right on the tail of a fat Me 110, filling my sights and an absolute sitter. I was about to fire and finish him when my Hurricane was hit from tail to cockpit by a blast from the 110's little friend, a 109 I had been too busy to notice... I reacted instinctively into a tight turn like a startled rabbit and went into a spiralling dive to get away from the 109, knowing there was damage but not how much... I tried to regain full control, but the Hurricane was hell bent downwards and was not answering the controls properly... I struggled to open my cockpit canopy, finding it jammed through damage... I remember I prayed for a miracle and it was answered as I felt the spin slowing and gradually we straightened out. I was at about 2,000ft... There was a grass airstrip ahead of me. The wheels dropped down and locked... I landed and taxied to a hangar and someone climbed on the wing to wrench open my canopy and help me out. The rear fuselage and tail of my sturdy Hurricane was tattered and torn. Once more I was grateful for the ruggedness of that machine. Soon an ambulance arrived and I was taken to hospital.'

Flight Lieutenant Donald 'Dimsie' Stones DFC and Bar, No 79 Squadron, 1940

Donald 'Dimsie' Stones

Donald 'Dimsie' Stones got his nickname when in 1940 he was caught with a book for five-year-olds, 'Dimsie goes to School'; it stuck for life! He flew Hurricanes with No 79 Squadron during the Battle of France, claiming five victories and one shared in one week, but was shot down on 14 May 1940. 'Dimsie' was still only 18 years old when he was awarded his first DFC! He remained with No 79 Squadron during the Battle of Britain and claimed a further four enemy aircraft destroyed, plus several 'probables'. On 7 September 1940 he was shot down by a Bf 109; he baled out with shrapnel wounds in his leg, but was back flying three weeks later. He was sent to Malta in July 1941, where he flew Hurricanes and was awarded a bar to his DFC. In May 1942 he arrived in India to command No 155 Squadron. Unfortunately, his command did not last long as he clashed with an Army Provost Marshal and was subsequently reprimanded for using bad language to the officer. He was demoted back to flight lieutenant and posted to join No 67 Squadron, at Chittagong on Hurricanes. On 15 May 1943 he was wounded by ground fire while leading an attack on a Japanese airfield. When he had recovered he was posted as a test pilot to units in Bombay and Karachi. In September 1945, now back in the UK, he lost an eye in a ground accident with a detonator. He subsequently joined the Colonial Service, serving in Africa and Malaya, and later sold and flew aircraft in Africa. He died in October 2002 aged 81.

‘There was no time for tears… ’

‘Sometimes there were hundreds of enemy aircraft and we were only 12 Hurricanes. We hoped and prayed that other squadrons had also been scrambled, but we never saw them. We just went ploughing in, picked our target and fought. You felt shots of adrenalin and you had a dry mouth… the natural worry about dying. Then back to the aerodrome and a safe landing, the groundcrew and the armourers smiling a welcome, particularly when the guns had been fired… The excitement, the casualties, the sorrow at the loss of a friend… Then back on readiness, waiting to go again. There was no time for tears, only sorrow, and off into the next scramble.’

Air Vice Marshal Harold ‘Birdy’ Bird-Wilson CBE DSO DFC and Bar AFC and Bar, No 17 Squadron, 1940

Left: No 17 Squadron pilots with Harold 'Birdy' Bird-Wilson's Hurricane P3878 YB-W. 'Birdy' is sitting on the tail.

Far Left: BBMF Hurricane LF363 in the colours of YB-W.

Below: Trying to relax on readiness.

Harold 'Birdy' Bird-Wilson

Harold 'Birdy' Bird-Wilson was involved in a crash in a training aircraft before the war; he suffered severe facial injuries and was operated on four times by plastic surgeon Archie McIndoe, thus becoming one of the first members of 'The Guinea Pig Club'. Having recovered, he joined No 17 Squadron in February 1940, flying Hurricanes, and fought during the Battle of France, sharing in the destruction of two enemy aircraft and damaging another. Over Dunkirk in May 1940 he damaged a Junkers Ju 87 and shared in the destruction of a Junkers Ju 88. During the Battle of Britain 'Birdy' claimed two enemy aircraft destroyed, three shared destroyed, two probably destroyed and one damaged. He was awarded the DFC, which ironically was gazetted on 24 September, the day that he was shot down in Hurricane P3878 'YB-W' over the Thames, by Adolf Galland. He baled out, injured and burned, was rescued by a MTB and admitted to the Royal Naval Hospital, Chatham. He recovered and after a period instructing at 56 OTU Sutton Bridge, he joined No 234 Squadron in March 1941 as a Flight Commander. In August he was rested again, spending seven months as an instructor at 52 OTU, before being given command of No 152 Squadron and later No 66 Squadron, both Spitfire units. After further rest periods and staff jobs, 'Birdy' was appointed as leader of the Harrowbeer Spitfire Wing on 9 June 1944, later moving to lead the Bentwaters Mustang Wing. His final wartime score was three destroyed, a share in a further six destroyed, three 'probables' and three damaged. In May 1945 he took command of No 1335 Jet Conversion Unit at Colerne. In a long post-war RAF career, he rose to the rank of air vice marshal and retired on 1 June 1974. He then worked for the aerospace industry. 'Birdy' Bird-Wilson died on 27 December 2000, aged 81.

Date	Aircraft Type	No.	Pilot, or 1st Pilot	2nd Pilot, Pupil or Passenger	Duty (Including Results and Remarks)	Single-Engine Aircraft Day Pilot (2)
—	—	—	—	—	Totals Brought Forward	
24.	Hurricane	P3878 W.	Self.	—.—	Patrol over Thames. Saw bombers going out over Eastchurch, after dropping their eggs on London. Do 17, Do 215 & He 111s (30). He 113's & Me 109's came down and started dog fight. Shot down!! Landed in the Thames by parachute.	1:30.
	"Taken to Haywards Heath Head Hospital" "Wounded by cannon shell and burns."					
	Rescued by M.T.B.-104					
	* End of Battle of Britain 2359 hours on 31st October 1940					
	Posted to No 56 O.T.U. Sutton Bridge					
7th	Hurricane.	L1910.	Self.	—.—	Air test.	10
7th	Master.	7884.	F/Lt Toyne	Self.	Experience on type.	20.
7th	Master.	7884	Self.	—.—	Landings on new type.	20
8th	Harvard.	N.7176.	F/Lt Toyne.	Self.	Experience on type.	25.
8th	Master.	7884.	Self.	P/O Tavener.	Wittering - Cranwell - S.B.	50.
9th	Hurricane.	3619.	Self.	—.—	Formation.	40.

Grand Total [Cols. (1) to (10)] 597 .. 40

Totals Carried Forward 60:50. 526:55. 2:10. 8:15. 6:30. 10:50 6:20.

No 17 Sqdns bag. 128 Jerries. for. 16 chaps.

Commanding officers No 17 Squadron
Jan 1937 C. Walter.
Nov 1939 AC Tomlinson
19 May 1940 J.H. Edwardes-Jones.
23 May 1940 G.D Emms.†
8 June 1940 R.I.G MacDougall
18 July 1940 C.W Williams†
29 Aug 1940 A.G Miller.

SHOT DOWN BY ME-109 IN THAMES ESTUARY (BLACK!!)

Membership No 01714.

SPECIALISING IN SAFETY PARACHUTES

Irving Air Chute of Great Britain, Ltd.

Directors: L. L. IRVIN (U.S.A.), F.R.Ae.S., F.R.S.A.; Group Capt. SIDNEY SMITH, D.S.O., A.F.C.; EDWARD S. SCEALES

ICKNIELD WAY, LETCHWORTH, HERTS, ENGLAND

Telephone: LETCHWORTH 888 (2 lines) Cable & Telegraphic Address: "IRVIN, LETCHWORTH"

23rd November, 1940.

For and on behalf of
IRVING AIR CHUTE OF GREAT BRITAIN LTD.,

for Managing Director.

DMS.
Enc. pin.

'Shot down by Me-109…'

Pilot's Flying Logbook entry
24 September 1940:

'Sept 24. Hurricane P3878 'W'. Patrol over the Thames. Saw bombers going out over Eastchurch, after dropping their eggs on London. Do-17, Do-215 and He-111s (30). He-113s & Me-109s came down and started dogfight… Shot down by Me-109. Landed in the Thames by parachute … Rescued by MTB 104 … Taken to Haywards Heath Hospital. Wounded by cannon shell and burns.'

Air Vice Marshal Harold 'Birdy' Bird-Wilson CBE DSO DFC and Bar AFC and Bar, No 17 Squadron, 1940

YB W

'Suddenly there was a blinding flash on my port wing… '

'We were attacked by Me 109s [sic] and, having made one attack on a 109, I was making a second at four who were well above when I realised that I would stall, so I levelled off. Suddenly, there was a blinding flash on my port wing and I felt a hell of a blow on my left arm, and then blood running down. I went into a hell of a dive and came back to Debden. A cannon shell had hit my wing and a bit of it hit me just above the elbow and behind. The shell had blown away most of the port flap so I tried to land without flaps. I could not stop and crashed into a pile of stones just off the field, hitting my face and cutting it in two places. I was taken to Saffron Walden General Hospital. They operated, but had to leave small pieces as it had penetrated the muscle.'

Pilot Officer Dennis Wissler, No 17 Squadron, 1940

Dennis Wissler

Dennis Wissler joined the RAF on a short service commission in July 1939. After completing his initial training he went to No 6 OTU at Sutton Bridge in late March 1940 to convert to Hurricanes. He was then posted to No 85 Squadron and subsequently to No 17 Squadron in France, until the unit was withdrawn to England on 19 June 1940, as France was overrun. Dennis Wissler shared in destroying a Heinkel He 111 on 29 July. He was wounded in the left arm in combat with a Messerschmitt Bf 109 over the Thames Estuary on 24 September and crashed on landing at Debden in Hurricane P3168. He was admitted to Saffron Walden Hospital, but by 10 October he was well enough to return to operational flying. On 11 November 1940 he was shot down by a Bf 109 whilst engaging Ju 87s attacking a convoy off Burnham. His Hurricane, V7570, crashed into the sea and he was reported 'missing'. Neither his aircraft nor his body were ever found and he is remembered on the Runnymede Memorial as one of those with no known grave. Dennis was only 20 years old and a few weeks earlier he had become engaged to be married to WAAF Operations Room 'Plotter', Edith Heap, then aged 21. She was on duty in the Debden Ops Room when her fiancée was killed and heard his fellow pilots call on the radio that he had gone down. Later, she sewed the pilot's wings from his best uniform onto the inside of her own uniform jacket so that they would always be against her heart.

Above: Of this group of No 17 Squadron pilots, only one was to survive the war. From left to right is: Plt Off Dennis Wissler (killed 11 November 1940), Plt Off Jack Ross (killed 6 January 1942), Flg Off Harold Bird-Wilson, Sqn Ldr Cedric Williams (killed 25 August 1940) and Plt Off David Leary (killed 28 December 1940).

GN
F
LF363

Tom Neil

Tom Neil joined the newly-reformed No 249 Squadron at Leconfield in May 1940, upon completion of his flying training. In mid-August, at the height of the Battle of Britain, the squadron moved south to Boscombe Down and then in September to North Weald. By the end of the battle, Tom had flown 141 combat missions, he had lost five Hurricanes 'one way or the other', his score stood at 10 enemy aircraft confirmed destroyed, plus two probably destroyed and one damaged. He was awarded the DFC on 8 October 1940 and a Bar to his DFC on 26 November. In May 1941 No 249 Squadron was sent to Malta. Tom Neil was now a flight commander. When he left Malta six months later his total score stood at 12 confirmed destroyed plus four shared. For the rest of the war he served as a tactics staff officer with 81 Group, an instructor with 56 OTU, Officer Commanding No 41 Squadron (Mk V and Mk XII Spitfires) and a liaison officer with the US 9th Air Force, with whom he flew P-51 Mustangs operationally over Europe before and after D-Day. In March 1945 he was posted to Burma where he undertook some operations with No I Wing, Indian Air Force, before returning to the UK in April. Tom Neil remained in the RAF after the war; he became a test pilot and then took command of No 208 Squadron in Egypt between 1953 and 1956, flying the Gloster Meteor jet fighter. After further staff tours he finally left the RAF as a wing commander in 1964.

Left: Hurricane LF363 in the colours of Tom Neil's GN-F.

'...two bodies flew past my head...'

'The familiar 'ack-ack' and line of bombers... Dorniers again. We were about the same height and not badly positioned. We curved towards them, climbing slightly... I concentrated on a Dornier out on the right and, with everything clicking into place, found myself dead astern, just below it and pitching about in its slipstream. Closing, I fired immediately and the whole of the port side of the German aircraft was engulfed in my tracer... Beside myself with excitement, I fired again, a longish burst, and finding that I was too close, fell back a little but kept my position. Then, astonishingly, before I was ready to renew my assault, two large objects detached themselves from the fuselage and came in my direction, so quickly, in fact, that I had no time to evade. Comprehension barely keeping pace with events, I suddenly recognised spread-eagled arms and legs as two bodies flew past my head, heavy with the bulges that were undeveloped parachutes. The crew! Baling out! I veered away, shocked by what I had just achieved.'

Wing Commander Tom Neil DFC and Bar AFC AE,
No 249 Squadron, 1940

Paul Farnes

Paul Farnes was born on 16 July 1918. He joined the RAF Volunteer Reserve in April 1938 and was mobilised in July 1939. He joined No 501 Squadron in September 1939 as a sergeant pilot and went with the unit to France in May 1940. He claimed his first victories during the Battle of France: a He 111 destroyed and two 'shared' kills against a He 111 and a Do 17. During the Battle of Britain flying from Gravesend and Hawkinge, he claimed five more enemy aircraft. In October 1940 he was awarded the DFM and was commissioned. In February 1941 he became an instructor with No 57 Operational Training Unit (OTU) and then, from November 1941, with No 73 OTU in Aden. Posted as a flight commander to No 229 Squadron (Mk IIC Hurricanes) in North Africa in February 1942, he flew with the squadron to Malta on 27 March 1942, later taking command of the unit. He returned to North Africa in late May 1942 and was then posted to Iraq, where he joined the RAF headquarters staff, remaining there until March 1945. On return to the UK he took command of No 124 Squadron, flying Spitfire Mk IXs, until the end of World War 2. An official fighter ace, Farnes' wartime score included seven and two shared destroyed, two 'probables' and 11 damaged. After the war he remained in the RAF until 1958; he commanded No 611 Squadron, equipped with Mustang IVs and served in staff appointments and instructional duties, eventually attaining the rank of wing commander. After retirement from the RAF, he returned to his civilian career in industry.

Right: No 501 Squadron pilots at readiness in 1940. Sgt Paul Farnes is third left seated.

'If you flew Hurricanes you were happy.'

Wing Commander Paul Farnes DFM AE

'I enjoyed it.'

'I have to admit that I did enjoy most of the Battle of Britain. After all, you've got to remember that we joined the RAF – I did and all the other Volunteer Reservists did – to fly. To be able to fly several times a day, every day, in one of the finest aeroplanes going, was good … and a bit of excitement thrown in as well. It was very fragile, but strangely enough it was a good life. I enjoyed it.'

Wing Commander Paul Farnes DFM AE

Left: Paul Farnes (middle) and No 501 Squadron pilots with a German souvenir in 1940.

Right: Hurricane LF363 bearing the code letters of Paul Farnes.

LF363
A
SD

MK356
UF
Q

SPITFIRE Mk IX MK356

Spitfire MK356 was one of a batch of Mk IX Spitfires built at the Castle Bromwich factory in early 1944. It was fitted with full-span wingtips and a Rolls-Royce Merlin 66 engine with a two-speed, two-stage supercharger optimised for low altitudes, making it a LF (Low Flying) Mk IXe. It was allocated to the recently-formed No 443 (Hornet) Squadron RCAF on 11 March 1944 and issued to 'B' Flight painted with the code letters '2I-V'.

No 144 Wing led a nomadic life over the next couple of months, perhaps in preparation for its 'expeditionary' role as part of the Second Tactical Air Force (2 TAF) in Europe after D-Day, leap-frogging from airfield to airfield, taking MK356 with it. Hutton-Cranswick, Westhampnett (Goodwood) and Funtingdon all hosted the Wing before it arrived at Ford on the Sussex coast on 14 May, which became its base until after D-Day.

In the period leading up to the invasion of France and just beyond, MK356 took part in fighter and fighter bomber operations over northern France, including tactical bomber escort and fighter sweep missions. The Spitfire flew 60 wartime sorties in a period of 60 days, during which it was damaged by enemy ground fire on three occasions. Indeed, a 1944 battle damage repair can still be seen on MK356's rear fuselage where a single German small-arms round entered low on the starboard side and exited high on the port side just ahead of the tail. In addition, the aircraft had to belly-land twice, but on each occasion it was rapidly repaired and was quickly back in action. MK356 was flown by a number of No 443 Squadron's pilots, but was the 'personal' aircraft of 21-year-old Canadian Fg Off Gordon Ockenden DFC from Edmonton, Alberta. Ockenden flew MK356 on 19 of its 60 wartime 'ops' and for some 40 of its total wartime flying hours of less than 100.

On D-Day, 6 June 1944, MK356 was flown on three beachhead cover patrols over the Normandy invasion beaches, two of them with Ockenden at the controls and each lasting approximately two hours. During another beachhead cover patrol on the afternoon of 7 June – D-Day+1 – Ockenden claimed a shared kill in MK356 against a German Bf 109, just off the Normandy coast (shared with Flt Lt Hugh Russel).

MK356 flew its final wartime sortie on 14 June, 'belly landing' back at Ford after the mission, because one of its main wheels had fallen off on take-off. No 443 Squadron deployed forward to France two days later to operate from Bazenville and MK356 was left behind to be collected by a Maintenance Unit. It was destined not to fly again for the next 53 years.

During the five decades that MK356 spent on the ground it remained in RAF hands. It was used as a training airframe and then as an RAF Station gate guardian in the open air at Hawkinge, Bicester and at Locking, where it was displayed in a flying attitude on a pole. It was also used as a static airframe for the filming of the movie 'Battle of Britain' in 1968, during which its wing main spars were damaged by some overzealous picketing. MK356 was then stored at Henlow until it joined the RAF Museum's Reserve Collection at St Athan in Wales.

During the late 1980s MK356 was surveyed with a view to the aircraft being restored to flying condition for the BBMF. The wings were found to be in poor condition, so it was decided to proceed with the restoration using the wings from the ex-Biggin Hill gate guardian Spitfire LF XVIe SL674, which had 'clipped' tips. The work started in January 1992 with a team of volunteers from St Athan. On 7 November 1997, MK356 took to the air again for the first time in over 53 years on its first post-restoration air test from St Athan, in the capable hands of the then OC BBMF, Sqn Ldr Paul 'Major' Day OBE AFC. A week later, on 14 November, he delivered MK356 to its new home with the BBMF at RAF Coningsby.

MK356 was returned to the full-span wing configuration during a major servicing in 2008 and now also flies with the later, pointed, so-called 'broad chord' rudder, which increases its crosswind limits for landing.

Left: BBMF Spitfire MK356 in the silver markings of UF-Q from No 601 Squadron.

'…I was never going to be crazy about this phase of our work…'

'The first time I saw my lean Spitfire with two bombs hanging on its slender wings, I decided that I was never going to be crazy about this phase of our work… During these few weeks before the invasion we flew hard on a wide variety of operations… A typical day's work might begin with dive bombing attacks against bridges and viaducts. After lunch we slung long-range tanks under the bellies of our fighters and roamed across France hunting for trains, transports and armoured vehicles. Perhaps our daily effort would end with dive bombing or strafing attacks against radar stations on the enemy coast.

'Sometimes we were switched from these pre-invasion tasks to dive-bombing attacks against V1 launching sites in the Pas de Calais. These were difficult targets to hit, because they were well camouflaged and heavily defended by flak… On the run-in you were bracketed by many bursts of heavy flak. Near the target the flak increased (along with my respect for the bomber boys who had to put up with this sort of thing on all their missions). When the target passed under the Spitfire's wing you waited for it to appear again behind it and then half rolled into a steep dive. As we plunged down the light flak came into its own. You released the bombs from about 4,000ft, braced yourself to take the 'g' and zoomed up again. The flak followed suit.'

Air Vice Marshal James 'Johnnie' Johnson CB, CBE, DSO and Two Bars, DFC and Bar

(This description of the work of No 144 Wing, by the Wing Leader, in the lead-up to D-Day describes the type of missions that Spitfire Mk IX MK356 flew. It also explains why MK356 was hit by enemy fire from the ground on three separate occasions.)

'Johnnie' Johnson

James 'Johnnie' Johnson joined the RAF Volunteer Reserve in 1939 as a sergeant pilot. He flew Spitfires during the Battle of Britain and then on offensive fighter sweeps in 1941 with No 616 Squadron, sometimes flying as Douglas Bader's wingman. In September 1941 he became a flight commander on the unit and then, on promotion to squadron leader, took command of No 610 Squadron. In March 1943 he was promoted to wing commander and given command of the Canadian Spitfire Wing at Kenley. In late 1943 he was rested from operations in a staff appointment at HQ 11 Group. Six months later he was again in command of a Canadian Wing of three Spitfire squadrons, this time No 144 Wing, which included No 443 Squadron RCAF with Spitfire Mk IX MK356 on it strength (now part of the BBMF fleet). He led the Wing during the build-up to D-Day and beyond, moving with it into France and then advancing through Belgium and into Germany. He was promoted to group captain in March 1945 and ended the war in command of No 125 Wing at Celle. 'Johnnie' Johnson is credited with being the highest scoring RAF fighter pilot of World War 2 with 34 confirmed and seven shared victories, three and two shared 'probables', 10 and three shared damaged and one destroyed on the ground. After the war he remained in the RAF, reaching the rank of air vice marshal as Air Officer Commanding Middle East Air Force. 'Johnnie' Johnson died on 30 January 2001, aged 85.

MK356

Charley Fox

Charley Fox joined the RCAF in October 1940 and, after training, spent two years as a flying instructor in Canada training hundreds of pilots. In 1943, he finally achieved his wish to become a fighter pilot. He arrived in England in August, and joined No 412 Squadron RCAF in January 1944 to fly Spitfires. Charley Fox led many ground attack sorties in the lead-up to D-Day, including three on the day of the invasion. On 18 June 1944, the squadron moved to B4 Advanced Landing Ground at Beny-Sur-Mer, in Normandy. During the summer offensive Charley Fox shot down two enemy fighters and damaged four others, but most of his sorties were against ground targets and he developed a reputation as a 'strafer'. Many of these sorties were flown in the face of intense anti-aircraft fire and on 14 different occasions the Spitfires he flew were damaged by ground fire. He was awarded a DFC for his 'exceptional courage and skill in pressing home his attacks against the enemy'. There has been much conjecture over the years as to which Allied fighter pilot caused Generalfeldmarschall Erwin Rommel, commander of the German forces in Normandy, to be removed from the war, by shooting his staff car off the road on 17 July 1944. Rommel sustained serious head injuries in the crash and in the days afterwards his survival was in doubt. He began to recover, but was then implicated in a plot against Hitler and was given no option but to commit suicide. There have been many Spitfire pilot claimants to the action that resulted in Rommel's demise, but modern research has led to it now being widely accepted that the Spitfire which attacked Rommel's car is most likely to have been flown by Charley Fox. By the time he was rested, at the end of January 1945, he had flown 224 operational sorties and he had been credited with destroying or damaging 22 locomotives and 153 vehicles in addition to claiming four enemy aircraft destroyed and five damaged. He was awarded a Bar to his DFC in February 1945. After the war he continued to serve in the peacetime RCAF with No 420 (Reserve) Squadron, flying Harvards, P-51 Mustangs and T-33 jets. In 1956, he began a career with a large shoe manufacturing firm, finally retiring in 1998. Charley Fox died at the wheel of his car on 18 October 2008, aged 88, while driving to attend lunch with his Harvard Association colleagues.

'… I saw hits on the car and I saw it start to go off the road'

'I saw this staff car coming along between lines of trees on a main road. I did a diving, curving strafe attack and I probably started firing at about 300 yards. I timed the shots so that I was able to fire and get him as the car came through a small opening in the trees. I got him on that pass. I was moving pretty fast, but I knew I got him. I saw hits on the car and I saw it start to curve and go off the road. At the time, I had no idea who it was… just a large black open car… gleaming in the sun without any camouflage, which was unusual.'

Squadron Leader Charles W. ('Charley') Fox DFC and Bar, CD (No 412 Squadron RCAF) 17 July 1944

'Aircraft on patrol on beach-head area. Heavy cloud conditions prevailing. No activity reported until squadron ready to leave. B Flight spotted four Me109s [sic] east of Caen. Bounced over Caen, one destroyed by F/L H. Russell shared with F/O G. F. Ockenden…'

No 443 Squadron RCAF Operations Record Book (F541) for 7 June 1944

(Gordon Ockenden was flying Spitfire Mk LF IXe MK356 '2I-V' when he claimed this shared kill on D-Day +1)

Gordon Ockenden

Gordon Ockenden from Edmonton, Alberta, joined the RCAF in April 1942, aged 18. After training and flying Hurricanes in Canada he was sent to England and joined the newly formed No 443 (Hornet) Squadron RCAF, which was equipped with Mk LF IXe Spitfires, including MK356, which bore the code letters 2I-V and which is now operated by the BBMF. No 443 Squadron was part of No 144 (Canadian) Wing, commanded by RAF fighter ace and renowned fighter leader Wg Cdr J. E. 'Johnnie' Johnson DSO and Bar DFC and Bar. In the build-up to D-Day, between 13 April and 4 June 1944, No 443 Squadron flew 487 operational Spitfire sorties on offensive operations. Gordon Ockenden remained with No 443 Squadron when it moved forward into France and then advanced towards Germany, until December 1944. By then he was a flight lieutenant credited with four confirmed aerial victories and one damaged, plus 35 vehicles destroyed on the ground. He was awarded the DFC on 18 December 1944. After the war Gordon Ockenden remained in the Canadian Air Force and retired as an air vice marshal. He died on 14 April 2000, aged 77.

'One day he's my tent mate; the next he's gone'

'One day he's my tent mate; the next he's gone. Art Horrell and I trained together in Canada. I attended his wedding. He and his wife had only a month together before we went overseas and joined No 443 Squadron in England. On 11 October 1944, we were at B-82 airfield at Grave in the Netherlands. Another pilot on the squadron, Paul Piche, flew Art to B-70, Antwerp, in an Auster, to collect a Spitfire to bring back. They wandered over the German lines and were shot down by 20mm flak near Deurne. Both were killed. I helped pack Art's stuff to send back to his wife. Of the 25 original pilots on the squadron, 11 didn't make it back home.

'Was it worth it? Yes, it was. We won. Just think about what the world would be like if we had lost.'

Air Vice Marshal Gordon Ockenden DFC CD
(flew BBMF Spitfire MK356 with
No 443 Squadron RCAF)

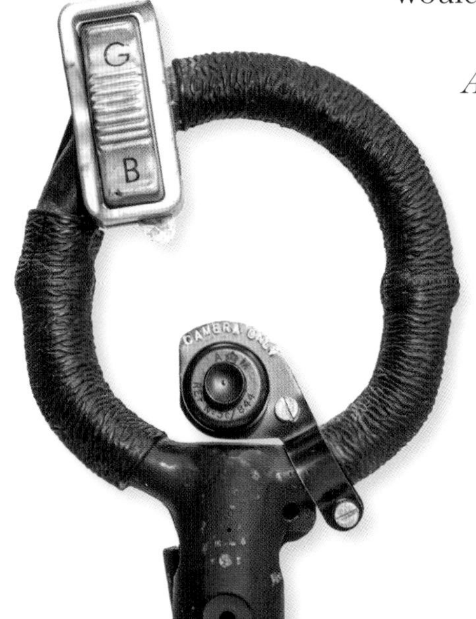

'...in a split-second of time, that Spitfire ceased to exist'

'I was leading a dive-bombing sortie, had just completed my own attack and was zooming up again, and at the same time watching the others dive down. My eyes were on one of them, descending vertically towards the target... when, in a split-second of time, that Spitfire just ceased to exist. I had never seen anything like it... At one moment there was the familiar, solid shape of a Spitfire; at the next, a flash, as though the aircraft had been vaporized and turned into a million pieces of confetti. It was the result of a bomb with a defective fuse detonating on the aircraft.'

Group Captain Sir Hugh 'Cocky' Dundas CBE, DSO and Bar, DFC (Wing Leader No 244 Wing, Italy)

Hugh 'Cocky' Dundas

Hugh 'Cocky' Dundas flew Spitfires with No 616 Squadron Auxiliary Air Force during the Battle of Britain and into 1941. After a brief period instructing, he became a flight commander with No 610 Squadron and then, on promotion to squadron leader at the age of 21, he took command of No 56 Squadron, the first unit to be equipped with the Hawker Typhoon. A year later he was promoted to wing commander and posted to the Mediterranean to lead No 324 Spitfire Wing from Malta and into Italy. In June 1944, whilst still only 23 years old, he was promoted to acting group captain and given command of No 244 (Spitfire) Wing, which included No 601 Squadron. One of the aircraft on the strength of '601' at this time was the silver Mk IX Spitfire MJ250 'UF-Q'. The Spitfires of 244 Wing were frequently engaged in dive bombing operations in support of the Allied advance through Italy. 'Cocky' Dundas' final wartime score was four destroyed, six shared destroyed, two shared 'probables', and 2½ damaged. Post war he made a successful career in the television industry and then with British Electric Traction. He was knighted in 1987. 'Cocky' Dundas died on 10 July 1995 aged 74.

UF

SPITFIRE PR Mk XIX PM631 & PS915

Left: The Flight's Spitfire PS915 in the colours of No 81 Squadron's PS852, a PR Mk XIX detached to Hong Kong in the early 1950s and flown by Flt Lt Edward 'Ted' Powles.

SPITFIRE PM631

Spitfire PR Mk XIX PM631 is thought to have been built at Reading in the spring of 1944 as a 'production prototype' of the high altitude photographic reconnaissance PR Mk XIX, fitted with a Rolls-Royce Griffon 66 engine and a pressurised cockpit. It was delivered to Southampton in May 1944 where it seems to have been used by the company for testing of PR Mk XIX components.

By March 1946 Spitfire PM631 was at RAF Benson, the RAF's 'hub' of photo-recce operations, where it remained until it was issued to No 203 Advanced Flying School in May 1949.

From June 1950 to June 1951, PM631 was stored at No 9 Maintenance Unit (MU) at Cosford, with only a brief temporary 'posting' to No 541 Squadron, based in Germany, for three weeks in early 1951.

After being modified for meteorological work, PM631 was leased to Short Bros from 2 July 1951. Based at Hooton Park, on the Wirral peninsula, and then at Woodvale, near Southport, Lancashire, it was flown by civilian pilots of the Temperature and Humidity Monitoring (THUM) Flight. This unit made daily ascents to 30,000ft to gather meteorological information.

On 11 July 1957, PM631 was flown to Biggin Hill from Duxford by World War 2 fighter ace Gp Capt Jamie Rankin, DSO and Bar, DFC and Bar, in formation with two other THUM Flight Mk XIX Spitfires, PS853 and PS915, to form the Historic Aircraft Flight, the forerunner of the BBMF.

PM631 has served with the BBMF ever since.

SPITFIRE PS915

Built at Southampton (Eastleigh) in 1945, Spitfire PR Mk XIX PS915 entered service just too late to see service in World War 2, being delivered to No 6 Maintenance Unit (MU) at Brize Norton on 17 April 1945. The aircraft was then transferred to Benson on 27 April, only 11 days before VE-Day. It was held at Benson until being allocated to No 541 Squadron on 21 June 1945. In July 1946, PS915 was moved to the Photographic Reconnaissance Development Unit, also based at Benson, to take part in tests of new cameras.

On 10 October 1946, Spitfire PS915 was allocated to the RAF Command in Germany, initially to RAF Luneberg until it joined No 2 Squadron at Wunstorf in April 1947. For the next four years, wearing the code letters 'OI-K' PS915 was operated by No 2 Squadron on 'Cold War' strategic reconnaissance sorties in connection with the East/West divide of Europe and during the politically tense period of the 1948-49 Berlin airlift.

PS915 was returned to the UK in 1951 and, after a period in storage at Cosford and having been suitably modified, it joined the Temperature and Humidity Monitoring (THUM) Flight at Woodvale in June 1954.

When the Historic Aircraft Flight, the forerunner of the BBMF, was inaugurated on 11 July 1957, PS915 became a founder member, being flown to Biggin Hill from Duxford by Wg Cdr Peter Thompson DFC. However, the aircraft was in poor shape and was quickly grounded. It subsequently served as a gate guardian at various RAF stations for many years.

In June 1984, PS915 was transported to the British Aerospace facility at Samlesbury for a full refurbishment to flying condition that was to include replacing the original Rolls-Royce Griffon 66 engine with an ex-Shackleton Griffon 58, which would, it was hoped, be easier to maintain with more readily available spares. PS915 eventually re-joined the BBMF in March 1987 after an absence of nearly 30 years.

HOOD JETTISON
PULL
GARMIN
WARNING
FLAPS MUST NOT BE
DOWN OR LOWERED
AT SPEEDS ABOVE
120KTS I.A.S.
OXY
PULL DOWN FOR NIGHT USE
KNOTS
R.P.M.
FUEL PRESSURE
WARNING
P.S.I.
BOOST
SIDE SLIP
SIDE SLIP
L
R
TURN
TURN
ALT
CHASSIS
OIL
RAD
ENGINE
ISOLATE
FUEL
FUEL
MAGNETO
MASTER
SWITCH
BRAKES
PORT
STARB
UP
NOSE
DOWN
CAUTION
MAIN TANKS
BOTTOM TANK
ONLY
S
ON
FUEL
OFF
R.P.M.
THROTTLE

When you're seven miles up in
the heavens
That's a hell of a lonely spot
And its fifty degrees below zero
Which isn't exactly hot
When you're frozen blue like
your Spitfire
And you're scared a green
shade of pink
When you're hundreds of
miles from nowhere
And there's nothing below but
the drink…

(Spitfire PR pilot's rhyme)

Ray Holmes

Ray Holmes joined the RAF Volunteer Reserve shortly after its formation in 1936. By 1940 he was a highly experienced fighter pilot flying Hurricanes with No 504 Squadron from Hendon airfield. In one of the most celebrated episodes of the Battle of Britain, the then Sgt Pilot Ray Holmes became something of an overnight hero when, out of ammunition, he rammed a Dornier Do 17 bomber over London, causing its destruction and being forced to bale out of his critically damaged Hurricane. When Fighter Command went on to the offensive in the spring of 1941, he flew fighter sweeps over occupied France. Subsequently, he was sent to Murmansk, Russia, with No 81 Squadron to instruct Soviet airmen on the Hurricane and also escorting Soviet bombers over German occupied territory. On his return from Russia, he qualified as a flying instructor and spent two years training future fighter pilots in the skills they would need to fly and fight. Ray Holmes then became a Spitfire photo-recce pilot, flying sorties with No 541 Squadron to photograph targets deep in Germany. Having somehow survived his wartime experiences, after the war he returned to his peacetime profession as a journalist in Liverpool and also built a reputation as a photographer. He lived life to the full and was playing tennis well into his eighties. Ray Holmes died on 27 June 2005, aged 90.

'...hurtling towards the enemy at 410 mph...'

'Twenty-nine thousand two hundred feet on the altimeter. Just under six miles up. Five hundred feet higher, and I would be making a dazzling white trail that would betray my position to every German fighter within 20 miles... The German radar had plotted me five minutes earlier when the first intermittent howl came over my radio. Gradually the moans merged into a steady note as their scanning beam swept to and fro, searching for my echoes, finding me and finally holding me.

'I had known loneliness many times in an aeroplane. But to be hurtling towards the enemy at 410mph was more than mere loneliness. It was desolation. As, with each minute, I probed seven miles further towards enemy territory, England seemed far behind indeed, and the chances of ever returning there grew remote... Guns, radar, aeroplanes, all sought me, manned by people with hatred in their hearts. They were out to destroy me, swiftly, utterly... I wondered what fate held for me in the next hour. Would I be intercepted, shot at, shot down? Would I have to bale out, be mortally wounded, or crash my Spitfire in flames? Would I die?

'My tour of ops on the sky-blue photographic Spitfire XIs and XIXs, though I could never have guessed it beforehand, was to be quite the toughest time of my war.'

Flight Lieutenant Ray Holmes (No 541 (PR) Squadron)

'...'I claimed one Fw 190 destroyed by an unarmed PR Spit XIX!'

'The flak at Koblenz was very heavy and intense, but inaccurate for height. I jinked before commencing the second photo run at 6,500ft. After covering the second target I climbed away and simultaneously sighted two Fw 190s to the south-west, above me, at 9,000ft. I opened up and climbed due west. One of the Fw 190s closed very quickly to 700 yards and began firing. I went into a tight spiral dive to zero feet, only just pulling out over trees, with the Fw 190 in pursuit ... The enemy aircraft failed to avoid the trees while pulling out; it blew up in the wood. I claimed one Fw 190 destroyed by an unarmed PR Spit XIX!'

Flight Lieutenant R.F.C. 'Chris' Garvey DFC and Bar
(No 541 Squadron photo-recce Spitfire pilot, March 1944 to February 1945)

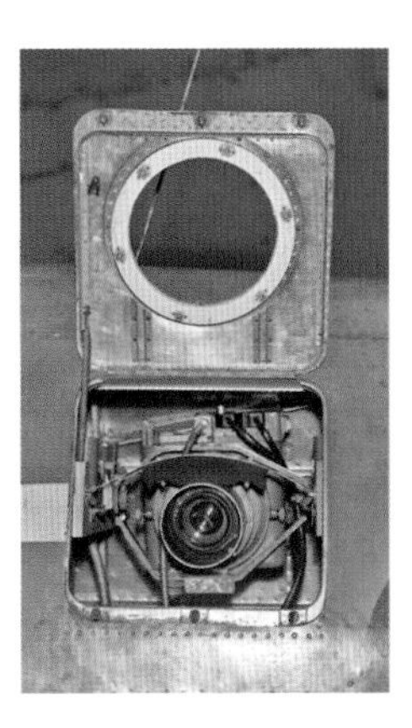

Chris Garvey

Chris Garvey from County Mayo, Ireland, was serving as an Army Second Lieutenant in the Royal Irish Fusiliers at the start of World War 2. Having answered a request for volunteers he was commissioned into the RAF in 1940. After completing his pilot training he was, perhaps unsurprisingly, posted to Army Co-operation Command, to fly the Allison-engined Mustang Mk I on tactical reconnaissance operations, initially with No 4 (ACC) Squadron and then with No 170 Squadron, where he was promoted to flight lieutenant and became the 'B' Flight Commander. He was awarded the DFC in February 1944 having flown 'a large number of photo-reconnaissance sorties' and for the 'courage and fighting spirit' he had displayed. In March 1944 he joined No 541 Squadron at RAF Benson to fly photo-reconnaissance Spitfire PR Mk XIs and, from May 1944, Griffon-engined Spitfire PR Mk XIXs. In November 1944 he was awarded a Bar to his DFC for completing numerous reconnaissance sorties over enemy territory and for the incident in which he claimed the destruction of the Fw 190 on 6 October 1944. Chris Garvey survived the war, but, tragically he was killed in a flying accident on a solo ferry flight in a de Havilland Mosquito NF30, when he crashed whilst approaching to land at RAF Shawbury on 14 January 1948.

Left: BBMF Spitfire PR Mk XIX PM631 representing a No 541 (PR) Squadron aircraft – a unit it actually served with – in the classic 'PR blue' colour and with D-Day invasion stripes.

'...should anything happen, I was on my own!'

'By the end of 1951, I had flown 63 PR sorties over Chinese territory. I was given "special" briefings for only four of them, each time being reminded that I had no authority to carry out the flights and, should anything happen, I was on my own!

'No one questioned when or where I flew, but on one occasion I was called into the office of the AOC Hong Kong, Air Commodore Bonham-Carter, who said to me: "Powles, I don't know what you are doing and I don't want to know, but if anything happens I won't be able to help you!"'

Flight Lieutenant Edward 'Ted' Powles AFC (flew clandestine photo-reconnaissance missions over Chinese territory from Kai Tak, Hong Kong, during 1951-52 in support of the Korean War)

Edward 'Ted' Powles

Edward 'Ted' Powles joined the RAF as an apprentice and trained as a photographer before becoming a pilot. He had a background in twin-engined aircraft and had never flown the Spitfire when he was posted without warning to complete a Spitfire 'Refresher Course' at RAF Finningley in January 1950. He then completed the photo-reconnaissance course at RAF Leuchars on Spitfire PR Mk XIXs. In August 1950 he was posted to RAF Tengah, in Singapore, where he spent four months flying photo-recce and strike sorties in Spitfire FR Mk XVIIIs, as part of Operation 'Firedog', the campaign against communist insurgents in Malaya. He was then transferred to No 81(PR) Squadron at RAF Seletar in late November 1950, from where he continued to fly a number of reconnaissance sorties over the Malayan jungle. He was then selected to lead a flight of two Spitfire PR Mk XIXs on a permanent detachment to RAF Kai Tak, in Hong Kong, departing on 1 January 1951. During 1951-52 Ted Powles flew a total of 107 secret, photo-recce flights over Chinese territory, many of them in Spitfire PR Mk XIX PS852. Some of these sorties were flown to the extreme range of the aircraft; on one occasion his engine stopped through lack of fuel just as he was landing and twice more he had insufficient fuel to taxy in after landing. He also famously climbed PS852 to a recorded 51,550ft in February 1952, a record altitude for a Spitfire. Ted Powles later emigrated to the US and died in 2008, aged 86.

VR A
KB726
KC A
PA474
THUMPER MK III

LANCASTER B1 PA474

Lancaster B1 PA474 was built at the Vickers-Armstrong Broughton factory on Hawarden airfield, near Chester, and was completed on 31 May 1945. The war in Europe had ended a few weeks earlier so the aircraft was modified for Far East operations against the Japanese as part of the 'Tiger Force' and was first flown in this configuration in August 1945. Combat operations in the Far East also ended before the aircraft could be deployed and instead it was delivered to No 38 Maintenance Unit (MU) at Llandow for storage, with just 3hrs 10min on the airframe.

Towards the end of June 1947, PA474 was flown to Armstrong Whitworth at Baginton, near Coventry, for conversion to PR1 standard for photographic reconnaissance work. The modifications included the removal of the gun turrets, the installation of a second pilot's position, the fitting of radar and the installation of cameras in the floor of the rear fuselage. The Perspex in the overhead cockpit canopy was replaced with metal panels, to protect against the high temperatures likely to be experienced overseas, and the Lancaster was painted silver. Following completion of these modifications PA474 returned to Llandow in early August 1947 and remained there until delivered to Benson for service with No 82 Squadron. From September 1948 to February 1952 PA474 conducted aerial survey mapping work in East and South Africa with No 82 Squadron, accumulating 2,000 airframe hours, before being returned to the UK.

The Lancaster was then loaned to Flight Refuelling Ltd at Tarrant Rushden with the intention of converting it into a pilotless target drone. PA474 was with the company for 19 months and underwent a major service prior to the proposed conversion. Fortunately, the drone conversion was cancelled by the Air Ministry before any actual physical work had been carried out – a Lincoln was used instead – and the Lancaster was saved from a fate which would almost certainly have prevented it from being with us today.

PA474 was, instead, allocated to the Cranfield College of Aeronautics, being flown there on 7 March 1954 by a civilian crew. At Cranfield the Lancaster was modified as a platform for the testing of various experimental aerofoil sections. It served in this capacity for the next ten years, which kept the aircraft airworthy, although it flew only some 100 hours during that time.

In April 1964 PA474 was grounded and adopted by the Air Historical Branch (AHB) for future display as a static exhibit in the proposed RAF Museum. Following the removal of all the experimental equipment she was flown to No 15 MU at Wroughton for initial restoration and the application of a wartime camouflage scheme. During this period PA474 also took part in two films, 'Operation Crossbow' and 'The Guns of Navarone'. Later in 1964 she was flown to Henlow for storage in the open air, to await the opening of the new museum.

At this point the commanding officer of No 44 Squadron – the first unit ever to be equipped with Lancasters – which was now flying Avro Vulcans at Waddington, sought and gained permission from the AHB for PA474 to be transferred into the care of the squadron. An inspection found that the aircraft was structurally sound and permission was granted for PA474 to make a single flight from Henlow to Waddington on 18 August 1965.

Over the next ten years the aircraft was refurbished, made fully airworthy and gradually restored to the condition and appearance of a wartime 'Main Force' bomber, with all its gun turrets back in place by 1975. The Lancaster joined the BBMF in 1973, initially at Coltishall, moving with the Flight to Coningsby in 1976.

PA474 was officially adopted by the City of Lincoln in 1975, and permission was granted for the aircraft to display the coat of arms and the name of the City on its nose, which it will always do, regardless of which wartime colour scheme it is painted in.

Today, PA474 is one of only two Lancasters in the world that remain in airworthy condition from 7,377 built; the other being Canadian Lancaster BX FM213 C-GVRA.

Left: The last two remaining airworthy Lancasters, with PA474 in the foreground.

Overleaf, left: PA474 has dual controls, whereas operational Lancasters were configured for and flown by a single pilot.

Overleaf, right: With the code letters 'WS-J', Johnnie Walker nose art, the slogan 'Still Going Strong', and an 'ops' log showing 106 missions, PA474 represented No 9 Squadron Lancaster W4964 between 1994-99.

PILOT

John Chatterton

John Chatterton was brought up on a farm in Lincolnshire. When war was declared, he was studying agriculture on a three-year BSc course at Nottingham University. As a farmer he could have qualified for reserved occupation status, but in 1940 he volunteered for the RAF. He passed the pilot aptitude tests, but failed the medical due to high-tone deafness, and so became an armourer. He continued to re-apply for aircrew and eventually passed the hearing test with an element of cheating. He trained as a pilot in the USA and the UK during 1942 and 1943 and subsequently joined No 44 Squadron at Dunholme Lodge, near Lincoln, in October 1943 as a Lancaster pilot and captain of his own crew. John and his men completed a full tour of 30 bombing 'ops' over occupied Europe, during a time when the odds against surviving were 4:1. He flew Lancaster ND578 KM-Y, 'Y-Yorker' on 15 of its first 18 'ops'; it eventually flew a total of 123 operations, becoming one of only 35 'centurion' Lancasters. John was awarded the DFC in April 1944. He finished the war and his time in the RAF with No 630 and then No 57 Squadrons at East Kirkby. After the war he returned to the family farm in Lincolnshire. He died in 2004, aged 84. John's son Mike became an RAF pilot and flew BBMF Lancaster PA474.

'What my gunners were reporting on this 'op' were, in fact, the deaths of over 50 bombers...'

'Both gunners had been reporting unusually large numbers of 'scarecrow flares', mostly off the port quarter and quite a way behind. 'Scarecrow flares' had first been mentioned at briefing some weeks earlier, with the explanation that the Germans were sending this impressive firework up to 20,000ft to look like an aircraft exploding and lower our morale. We hardened cynics were pretty sure that they were exploding aircraft, but knowing nothing of the German night fighters using upward-firing, tracer-less cannon, we could not understand why there was not the usual exchange of tracer in the normal 'curve of pursuit'. What my gunners were reporting on this 'op' were, in fact, the deaths of over 50 bombers. That night, Me 110 and Junkers 88 night fighter squadrons had been pulled in from the north and south to orbit fighter beacons near Bonn and Frankfurt. They could hardly believe it when they found the main bomber stream flying en masse between the two beacons and into their waiting arms, like gentleman guns in a partridge shoot waiting for the coveys to sweep over them. The resulting slaughter was much the same.'

Flight Lieutenant John Chatterton DFC (Lancaster pilot who flew a full tour of 30 'ops' with No 44 Squadron)

Above: The Flight's Lancaster in the colours of No 460 Squadron.

Right: A Lancaster is loaded with a 4,000lb 'Cookie' bomb in November 1943.

NAVIGATOR

Don Charlwood

Don Charlwood was born in Melbourne, Australia, in September 1915. He joined the RAAF in 1940 and sailed for Canada in 1941 to train as a navigator. He was eventually posted to No 103 Squadron at Elsham Wolds, in North Lincolnshire, in the autumn of 1942, having crewed up with an Australian pilot and wireless operator and an otherwise British crew. The squadron had just re-equipped with the Lancaster. Don was now aged 27, older than most who flew the bombers. In the seven months during the winter of 1942-43 whilst he was flying with No 103 Squadron, Don's crew was the only one to complete a full tour of 30 operations. Of the 20 men from his training course who qualified as navigators with him, only five survived the war. At the end of his tour with No 103 Squadron, he was commissioned and became an instructor at No 27 OTU, a bomber training unit at Lichfield. In February 1944 he was repatriated to Australia, where he served for the rest of the war. On his return to civilian life, Charlwood worked for 30 years as an air traffic controller. He also wrote several books, including 'No Moon Tonight' recounting his wartime experiences as a Lancaster navigator. He died in June 2012, aged 96.

'...Navigator where the hell are we?'

'On the return journey from our target at Mannheim, about an hour out, I took an astro-navigation fix, which showed us about 40 miles south of track. I regarded this fix with extreme doubt. Getting another fix was then complicated by the development of high cloud obscuring the stars. Our Gee set and our radios were both out of order and, in any event, we were beyond the range of the British transmitters. I continued with dead reckoning navigation for almost two hours. For all that time a stronger than forecast wind blew us further south of track. There was still cloud above and below us and no sight of the ground when there was a cry from the rear turret, "Flak, dead astern!" I jumped to my feet. We should by now have crossed the English coast. "Flak coming straight up" called the rear gunner. We swung away from it and the pilot called on the intercom, "Navigator, where the hell are we? When we get out of this muck what about a bit of astro?" I shuffled to the astrodome and raised my head into the Perspex bubble. I could hear on the intercom, the pilot and the flight engineer discussing how little fuel we had remaining. "I am to blame for our predicament", I thought, "for throwing away the lives of our crew". I realised that my chief fear of ops had been this, the fear of wasting the lives of other men who were relying on me... Somehow we reached Waddington, our six hours of fuel stretched to seven hours forty-five minutes.'

Flight Lieutenant Don Charlwood RAAF
(Lancaster navigator who flew a full tour of 30 'ops' with No 103 Squadron)

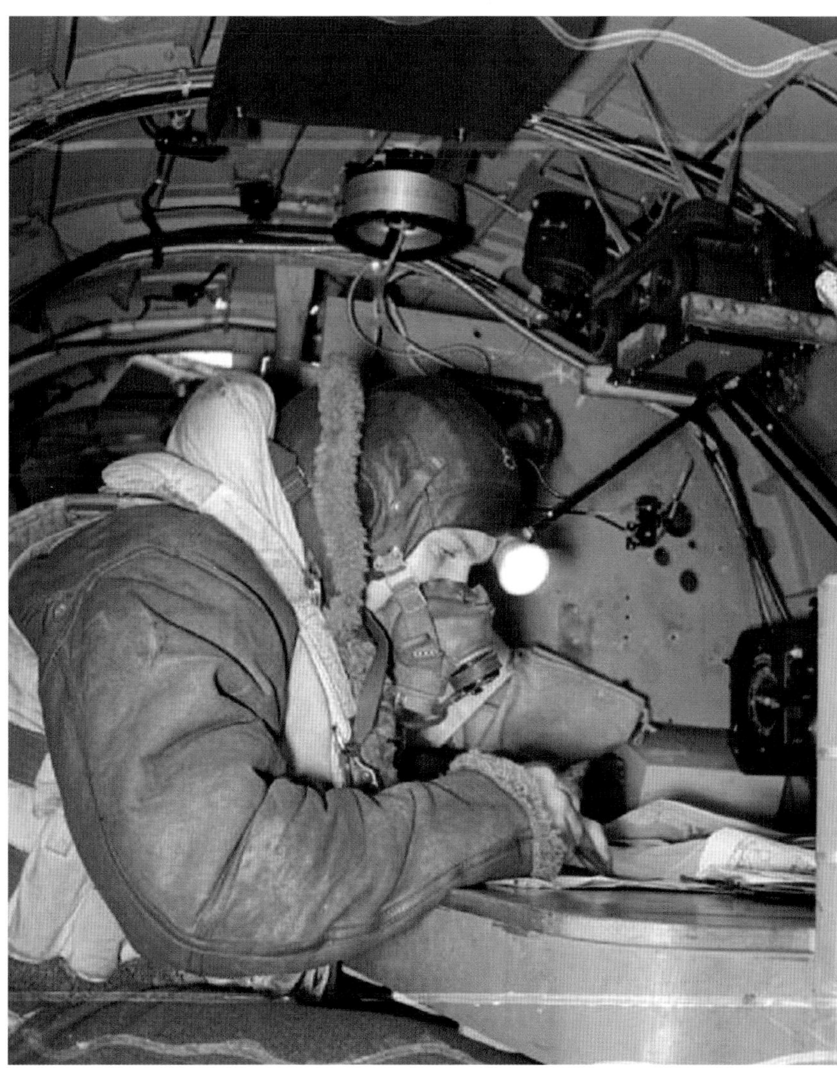

BOMB AIMER

John Bell

John Bell initially trained as an observer before becoming a bomb aimer, crewing up with pilot Bob Knights (later Flt Lt Knights DSO DFC). The crew joined No 619 Squadron at Woodhall Spa in June 1943 and during the so-called Battle of Berlin they made the long and dangerous trip to the Big City and back on eight occasions. As the Lancaster had only a single pilot, Bob Knights decided that the bomb aimer could be best spared from his other duties should the pilot be killed or incapacitated and he trained John to fly the aircraft back over England in such an eventuality. Many of the crew's 'ops' with No 619 Squadron were flown in a Lancaster coded 'PG-T' and named *Thumper Mk II*. As the crew approached the end of their tour with No 619 Squadron they decided to volunteer for a second operational tour with No 617 Squadron as they thought it was safer to stay together rather than be split up. They joined '617' in January 1944. John flew a total of 50 wartime 'ops', 27 of them in No 617 Squadron Lancaster DV385 which the crew named *Thumper Mk III*, before electing to opt for ground duties, as was his right. He became an accounts officer and later a photographic interpreter serving in the Korean War. At the time of publication John was 94 years old and living in West Sussex.

Right: PA474 as Thumper Mk III *of No 617 Squadron.*

'…I was able to watch the Tallboy all the way down…

'As bomb aimer I was right up front in the nose. I'm 6ft 4in and it was pretty cramped, but you had a good view through 180 degrees. On 17 July 1944 we attacked the V-2 rocket site at Wizernes in the Pas-de-Calais area of France, dropping Tallboy bombs on the 150ft diameter concrete dome. Our 617 Squadron Lancasters had the special Stabilising Automatic Bomb Sight (SABS) and the pilot had to maintain straight and level, and a steady speed, for about 10 minutes on the approach, so that it could make the calculations. If there was any flak you just had to ignore it, but the real problem was cloud as you had to be able to see the target to track it in the bomb sight. Fortunately, it was clear that day. When everything was going right there was no need for communication between the bomb aimer and the pilot, as the Bomb Direction Indicator mounted in front of the pilot gave him all the steering information needed. It was only if that drifted off that the bomb aimer needed to give the pilot heading corrections to make the pilot's indication live again. At Wizernes I was able to watch the Tallboy all the way down to impact and I was elated when it hit the north-west edge of the dome. I shouted out "bullseye"… We had a celebration that night.'

Wing Commander John Bell MBE DFC (bomb aimer who flew Lancaster DV385 Thumper Mk III *with No 617 Squadron)*

An RAF Lancaster silhouetted during a raid over the German city of Hamburg.

FLIGHT ENGINEER

Jim Leith

Jim Leith applied to join the RAF shortly after his 18th birthday in 1941. Despite asking to be an air gunner he was trained and employed as an airframe mechanic and served at Biggin Hill and Manston, before becoming an airframe fitter. In March 1943 he was offered the opportunity to become a flight engineer and jumped at the chance. He received his flight engineer's brevet in early June 1944. He crewed up with Frank Mouritz's crew at the Heavy Conversion Unit at Swinderby later that month and the crew subsequently joined No 61 Squadron at Skellingthorpe in September 1944. Their first five operations were flown in veteran Lancaster EE176 *Mickey the Moocher*, before it was retired having flown a total of 130 operations. The crew eventually completed 34 'ops' by April 1945 when Jim was posted to be an instructor. After being 'demobbed' in August 1946 he returned to the company who had employed him pre-war from the age of 14, and worked his way up from accounts clerk to company secretary. In 1970 he moved to another company where he eventually became the managing director. He retired in 1987. Jim Leith died in April 2009 aged 86.

'We were hit several times with cannon shells…'

'On our way home we were attacked from below by a Ju 88 night fighter with an upward-firing cannon. Fortunately, our mid-upper gunner spotted the enemy aircraft flying beneath us and shouted for the pilot to corkscrew. We had just started the corkscrew to starboard, which begins with a violent banking, diving turn, when the Ju 88 opened fire. We were hit several times with cannon shells along the starboard wing and some considerable damage was caused to our old *'M' for 'Mickey'*. Had the corkscrew started a few seconds later, the pilot and I, the navigator and the bomb aimer, all being in the cockpit area adjacent to the wing which received the cannon shell hits, would probably not be here today… While this was happening, both gunners were firing back, the mid-upper gunner spraying tracer bullets all over the sky around us. The rear gunner, however, was more accurate and scored hits on the Ju 88. It dived away from us on fire.'

Sergeant Jim Leith (Lancaster flight engineer with No 61 Squadron, who was part of the crew of Flying Officer Frank Mouritz RAAF, which flew Lancaster EE176 Mickey the Moocher*)*

WIRELESS OPERATOR

'Lish' Easby

Lishman 'Lish' Easby joined the RAF in 1941 and initially served as a ground wireless operator before training as a wireless operator air gunner. He joined Ron Clark's all-NCO crew at No 28 Operational Training Unit (OTU) at Wymeswold at the end of May 1943 and they were then posted to No 100 Squadron at Waltham, near Grimsby. Shortly after joining the squadron and despite being a 'sprog' crew, they were allocated a brand-new Lancaster, EE139, which they named *Phantom of the Ruhr*. The crew flew their first 'op' on 11 June 1943, taking 'The Phantom' to Dusseldorf and back. They completed 23 'ops' in EE139, including two to Italy, before it was badly damaged on their sortie to Mannheim on 23 September 1943 – 300 shrapnel holes were later found in the Lancaster – and it had to be taken in for extensive repairs. The crew completed a further four 'ops' together, the last of those after having been transferred to No 625 Squadron at Kelstern. The crew was then 'screened' and disbanded. Lish was posted to be an instructor at the OTUs at Tilstock and then at Sleap. He then joined Transport Command and flew Halifaxes with No 298 Squadron, spending time in India and Northern Burma. He was eventually demobbed in 1946 as a flight lieutenant and spent the rest of his working life as a civil servant.

'...there seemed little chance of ever seeing England again...'

'Of our 23 ops with 'The Phantom', the most eventful was our last with her to Mannheim on 23 September 1943. Over the target we were picked up by a master searchlight beam; the pilot immediately took evasive action, but the searchlight held us. This was joined by others and soon we were coned in searchlights, a sitting target for flak and fighters. Every gun in Mannheim seemed to be firing at us. As we were now right over the target the pilot opened the bomb-doors and the bomb aimer released the bomb load. We received two direct hits by anti-aircraft shells. The first passed through the bomb bay and out the top of the fuselage without exploding. The aircraft went into a spiral dive, the pilot's control column was jammed hard over and it took the combined strength of both the pilot, Ron Clark, and the flight engineer, 'Benny' Bennett, to regain control and pull out. Afterwards we discovered that the cable to the starboard aileron had been severed. We lost height from 25,000ft down to 8,000ft and were still in the searchlights. We were also attacked by a night fighter, but we were blinded by searchlights and neither air gunner could respond. At some point, we received a second hit by flak this time on the starboard tail plane. The whole aircraft was now vibrating violently and there seemed little chance of ever seeing England again. I donned my parachute and waited for the order to abandon aircraft. The starboard tail plane and fin were flapping like a bird's wing, threatening to separate from the aircraft. Benny, our flight engineer, came to the rescue. He cut the cable to the starboard aileron trim tab and the aircraft settled down, allowing us to return to Waltham for an emergency landing. We were lucky to get back and the fact that we did was mainly due to the skills of the pilot and the engineer. Shortly after the raid, Ron was awarded an immediate DFC and Benny the DFM.'

Flight Lieutenant Lish Easby (Lancaster Wireless Operator with No 100 Squadron, who was part of the crew of Flight Lieutenant Ron Clark DFC, which flew Lancaster EE139 HW-R Phantom of the Ruhr *on 23 'ops')*

HW P

MID-UPPER GUNNER

Russell Margerison

Russell Margerison from Blackburn, Lancashire, was just 17 when he joined the RAF to train as an air gunner. On his 21st 'op' in May 1944 his Lancaster was shot down, Russell and four other members of the crew baled out and survived, but the pilot and flight engineer were both killed. Russell Margerison was assisted by the Belgium Resistance, hidden in the home of a millionairess, then betrayed to the Gestapo and marched off to a prisoner of war camp at Bankau in Poland, all before he was 20 years old. The camp was eventually liberated by the Soviet Army and he joined thousands of refugees on the long march home, eventually reaching Britain in May 1945. After the war, he worked as a newspaper compositor, first for the Blackburn Times and later for the Lancashire Evening Telegraph. He then moved on to the Manchester Evening News, later becoming a sub editor, where he spent many years until his retirement. He died on 4 October 2014, aged 90.

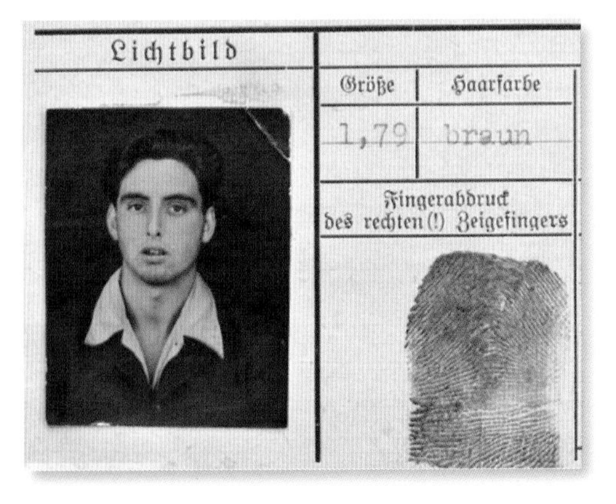
Lichtbild
Größe | Haarfarbe
1,79 | braun
Fingerabdruck des rechten (!) Zeigefingers

Above: The POW identity papers of Russell Margerison.

'Abandon aircraft. Abandon aircraft!'

'On the return flight from the Ruhr at 23,000ft there was a sudden heavy rattle of cannon and vicious, sparkling white tracer whipped through us. The Lanc appeared to stop dead, as if to gasp for breath, then lurched on like a drunken man. Both port engines were ablaze and flames spewed back over the port tail plane and fin. Down went the nose of the aircraft, the engines screaming in agony… "Abandon aircraft. Abandon aircraft!" Shocked at the suddenness and speed at which events were moving, I watched as curls of metal rolled off the huge oval tailfin and revealed the framework underneath. Off came my gloves. I uncoupled my oxygen supply and electrically heated suit, then vacated the turret in record time. The whole fuselage was an inferno. Flames licked at my parachute, which lay on the floor. I grabbed it and tried to hook it on to the harness I was wearing. I failed. Smoke and lack of oxygen were making breathing difficult as I tried, and failed, once again to clip on the 'chute. The heat was intense, ammunition was exploding. Through holes made by the cannon shells, I could see flames outside. In sheer desperation, I banged on the 'chute as I tried to attach it again. This time it stayed on, and I rushed to the door. As soon as I poked my head outside, I was whipped out of the plane by a fierce wind. As I floated down it was a grim sight, watching our plane curl ever downwards, streaming flame as she went. I had seen many Lancs go down, but this was different. Some of my mates could well be inside this aircraft. The Lanc hit the ground, leaving a circle of fire. I turned my head away.'

Sergeant Russell Margerison (Lancaster mid-upper gunner with No 625 Squadron)

LEADER
AR L
PA474

James 'Col' Challis

'Col' Challis was born in New South Wales, Australia, on 6 August 1923, and enlisted in the Royal Australian Air Force (RAAF) in April 1942, aged 18. He trained in Australia as a Wireless Operator/Air Gunner and embarked on a troopship to the UK in March 1943. Initially, Sgt Challis was posted to a Boulton Paul Defiant squadron as an air gunner in the aircraft's four-gun turret. When the Defiant was withdrawn from front line service not long after, he re-mustered to Bomber Command and joined a crew captained by the then Sgt Jerry Bateman RAAF, as the mid-upper gunner. After the crew had completed the necessary training and conversion courses they joined No 460 Squadron (RAAF) at RAF Binbrook on the Lincolnshire Wolds. In early August 1943 the crew took on Lancaster BIII W5005, AR-L 'Leader', with its colourful kangaroo nose art, as their individual aircraft. They flew W5005 for the first time on their second operation, a raid against Mannheim, on 9 August 1943. Challis completed 22 of his tour of 33 'ops' with No 460 Squadron in W5005, including two bombing raids on Milan in Italy, and four successful 'ops' to Berlin. He said that the crew were forced to evade German night fighter attacks on 11 occasions. After completing his first full tour of 'ops' – something few survived – Challis volunteered for a second tour and flew a further 21 'ops' in Handley-Page Halifaxes with No 466 Squadron RAAF, after which he was awarded the DFC. When the war in Europe ended Challis was posted to the 'Tiger Force' which was, in fact, never needed to deploy to the Far East. He returned to Australia and remained in the RAAF or the Reserves for a total of almost 37 years. He died in Australia some years ago.

Left: The Flight's Lancaster as No 460 Squadron's AR-L 'Leader'.

'I could see the white scarf around the German pilot's neck.'

'In a lot of cases the mid-upper gunner saw an enemy aircraft before the rear gunner. Up on top you had a terrific view. One night we were over Berlin. It was a cloudy night and they were sky marking the target. There were lots of flares and things around. Suddenly I spotted this Me 109 [sic], I'd say about 50 yards away. He hadn't seen us, he banked and I could see the white scarf around the German pilot's neck. I was already sort of thinking about a DFM! I squeezed the triggers and all I got was two clicks. Both my guns were frozen up! I could see the white scarf around him and he didn't see us, and he just banked away and was gone.'

Flying Officer Colin James 'Col' Challis DFC RAAF (No 460 Squadron mid-upper gunner in Jerry Bateman's crew flying Lancaster W5005 AR-L 'Leader')

REAR GUNNER

James Flowers

Horace James Flowers (known as James) enlisted in the RAF in March 1944 and trained as an air gunner at Stormey Down, South Wales. He had already met fellow trainee gunner Henry J. Flowers. The two Flowers became best friends and served together in the same Lancaster crew with James in the rear turret and Henry in the mid-upper. James was one of only two Englishmen in the crew, which also included three New Zealanders, a Scotsman and a Welshman. The crew was posted to No 50 Squadron at Skellingthorpe, just west of Lincoln, in January 1945. They flew their first 'op' on 5 March 1945 and completed a total of 10, action-packed, bomber 'ops' before the war in Europe ended. They were then transferred to No 44 Squadron at Spilsby, as part of the 'Tiger Force' which was preparing to deploy to the Far East, but Japan's capitulation in August 1945 rendered it unnecessary. James was finally discharged from the RAF in 1947. After the war he became a driving examiner.

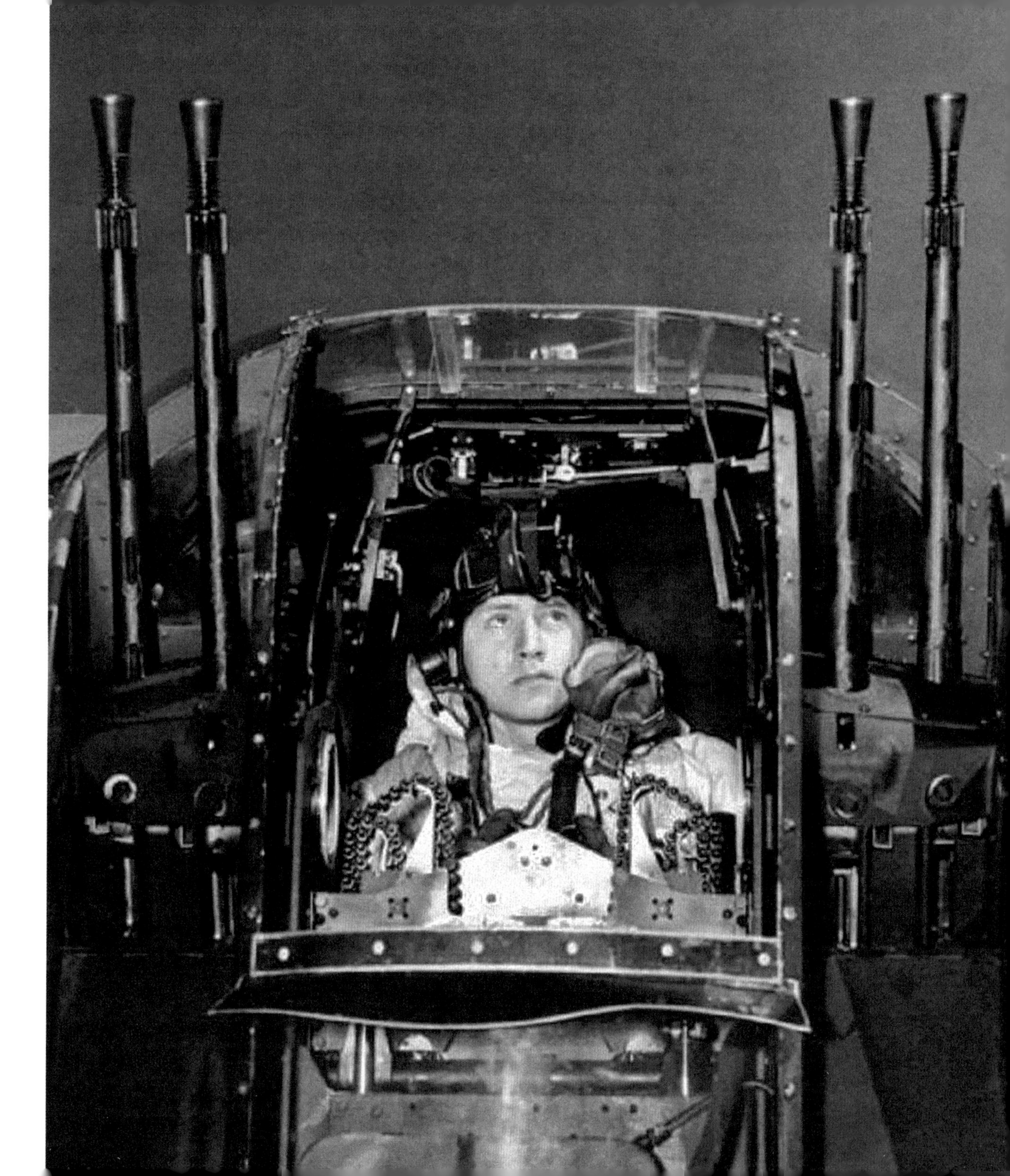

‘Pressing my firing button I fired a prolonged burst…

‘Two hours after take-off, pitch dark, as I watched the engine exhaust sparks of a Lanc drift gently from port underneath us, there was a tremendous explosion just behind. Two Lancs had collided. The large flash of light then split apart and seconds later there were two big flashes as both aircraft blew up nearly taking us down with them. Sadly, I realised that 14 airmen had just lost their lives. Those unseen bombers in the dark now seemed very menacing. At 12,000ft with a moonlit sky the 10/10th cloud cover 2,000ft below us seemed like a rolling sea. Suddenly, to our starboard rear a small dot appeared from the clouds. It looked for all the world like a fly. “It’s a fighter. It’s a fighter”, I thought. I trained my guns on the object as it slowly gained height, moving to a position dead astern of me. The hours spent in training, viewing silhouettes of all types of aircraft, paid off as I recognised a Me 109 [sic]. Now, with my gun sight filled, it had reached firing range. Pressing my firing button I fired a prolonged burst and my four .303 machine-guns began rattling away as I watched their tracer bullets fly straight into the enemy fighter. Instantly, as if out of control, it dived vertically into the cloud cover beneath us. “Got him”, I thought. Back at base I claimed a probable.’

Flight Sergeant H. James Flowers

(Lancaster rear gunner with No 50 Squadron on his first ‘op’ on 5 March 1945 to Bohlen, Germany)

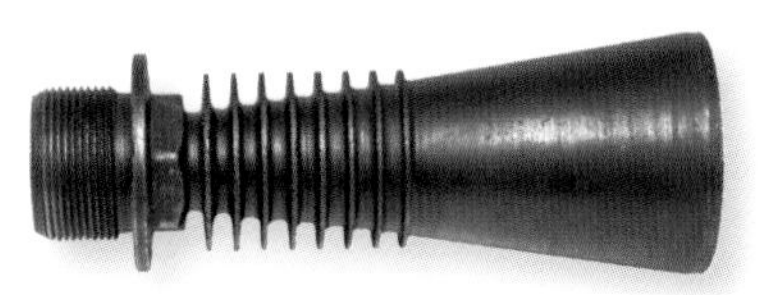

Below: Lancaster R5689 VN-N of No 50 Squadron starting its engines at RAF Swinderby in August 1942.

'...my logbook was floating in front of me!'

'When a searchlight picks you up, it's like being in broad daylight. You could see everything inside the aircraft. You had to corkscrew to get out of it. Well, 'Dougy' Millikin was very good at that! The routine was diving, rolling, climbing, rolling, diving, rolling, and my logbook was floating in front of me!'

Warrant Officer John Tait (Lancaster Wireless Operator in the No 50 Squadron crew of Flying Officer 'Dougy' Millikin DFC [left], whose aircraft, LL922, was coded 'VN-T')

VN
T
PA474
City of Lincoln

LEADER

‘No enemy plane will fly over the Reich territory’

Reichsmarschall
Herman Göring

'THE LAST!'
PS915
UF
Q
MK356
P7350
4D
V
TE311

SPITFIRE Mk LF XVIe TE311

Spitfire Mk LF XVIe TE311 was manufactured, as all Mk XVI Spitfires were, at the Castle Bromwich Aeroplane Factory. It was built as a low-back, clipped-wing Packard Merlin 266-powered LF XVIe during 1945 and was delivered to No 39 Maintenance Unit (MU) at Colerne, on 8 June, exactly one month after VE Day.

With the war in Europe at an end, TE311 was placed in storage until it was allocated to the Empire Central Flying School Handling Squadron at Hullavington on 5 October 1945. TE311 served on the unit's strength until mid-February 1946 when it was delivered to No 33 MU at Lyneham.

On 31 May 1951, TE311 was placed on charge with No 1689 Ferry Pilots Training Flight at RAF Aston Down. However, only three weeks later, on 21 June, the aircraft suffered an accident when the starboard tyre burst on landing. TE311 did not fly again until December that year. In July 1952 the Spitfire was transferred to the Ferry Training Unit at RAF Benson, continuing in the same role, until it was returned again to No 33 MU for storage.

On 13 December 1954, having flown only some 30 hours total, TE311 was transferred to non-effective stock, grounded but still in RAF hands. Then on 8 August 1955, TE311 was allocated to RAF Tangmere as a 'gate guardian', on display at the Station's main gate. After 12 years of standing outside in the elements, TE311 was loaned to Spitfire Productions Ltd for use in the making of the epic film 'Battle of Britain'. It was restored to taxying condition and modified with a false 'high-back' rear fuselage, in keeping with Battle of Britain era Spitfires, so it could be used in ground scenes in the film. When its brief spell as a 'movie extra' was over, TE311 was returned to its normal configuration and in August 1968 it became a 'gate guardian' at RAF Benson, where it spent the next four-and-a half years.

At the end of January 1973, TE311 was allocated to the RAF Exhibition Flight based at RAF Bicester and later, from 1976, at RAF Abingdon. For many years the Spitfire toured the country by road, visiting shows as a static exhibit, in company with Spitfire Mk XVI TB382. Both airframes were crudely modified for ease of dismantling, loading, transport and reassembly, with the aircrafts' wings being regularly removed and refitted.

In 1999, the RAF announced that the two Exhibition Spitfire Mk XVIs were to be put up for disposal. However, after some high-level negotiations and with the BBMF pointing out that these were RAF aircraft that could be a useful source of spares within the Service, TE311 and TB382 were delivered to RAF Coningsby for 'spares recovery'. Subsequently, TB382 was broken up for spares and struck off charge, but inspection of Spitfire TE311 by the BBMF engineers showed that it was in a fairly good state of preservation and, whilst much work was required and many parts were missing, it could be a candidate for restoration to flying condition. BBMF engineer Chief Technician Paul Blackah MBE took the lead in this decision and in the restoration, aware that this would give the BBMF a sixth flying Spitfire of a mark not then represented in the fleet, but a type that the Flight had once before operated in its very early days.

The restoration of TE311, which began in June 2002, initially had no official backing or funding, not least because this was supposed to be a 'spares recovery' programme. Work was carried out in the volunteer team's own time, over lunch breaks, after the working day had ended and at weekends, but eventually it was agreed that TE311 would officially be placed on the strength of the BBMF.

Spitfire TE311 took to the skies once again on Friday 19 October 2012, for the first time in over 58 years, in the capable hands of Sqn Ldr Ian Smith MBE, the then OC BBMF. Not surprisingly, there were some teething problems to iron out, but TE311 was ready and available to play a full part in the 2013 BBMF display season, giving the Flight an additional airworthy Spitfire and one with quite a different look from the others. Since then, this Spitfire has become a stalwart of the Flight and a favourite amongst the BBMF fighter pilots.

Left: BBMF Spitfires in echelon, headed by TE311.

‘I saw to my surprise… the unmistakable shape of a V-2 rocket that had just been launched’

‘The principal job of No 602 Squadron with our Spitfire 16s was to make life as difficult as possible for the German V-2 operators. We were withdrawn from Antwerp to Coltishall in Norfolk, and our ‘parish’ was the whole of the coastal strip of Holland from the Hook to Den Helder. We dive-bombed, skip-bombed and strafed railways, roads, bridges, anything that moved, and we also attacked suspected V-weapon launching sites that were reported to us by the Dutch Resistance workers.

‘On one occasion (my logbook tells me it was 14 February 1945) I led such an attack. We carried 1,000lb of bombs on our Spit 16s, and we dive-bombed a V-2 site in a wood just north of The Hague. I think I must have been feeling particularly aggressive, because after delivering the bombs, we turned back in to strafe the anti-aircraft gunners that had been shooting at us. As we returned to this target, I saw to my surprise, at a distance of about 600 yards, the unmistakable shape of a V-2 rocket that had just been launched, rising into the air very slowly, from the forest we had just bombed, right in front of us. It was an incredible sight and, of course, no-one had ever seen one until that time, or certainly none of my little lot. It was so unexpected that I couldn’t do much about it, because I was having a rather unpleasant argument with these gentlemen on the ground, but my number four, a little Scotsman called ‘Cupid’ Love [Flight Sergeant Tommy Love], who was away out and low to my right, actually fired at this V-2 in flight, as it went up straight through the ring of his gun sight. I think this must have been one of the most optimistic shots of the entire war and probably the only occasion in which an airborne ballistic missile was engaged by a conventional aircraft. I dread to think what would have happened if he’d hit the thing. He’d have blown us all up!’

Flight Lieutenant Raymond ‘Bax’ Baxter OBE (‘A’ Flight Commander, No 602 (City of Glasgow) Squadron, Auxiliary Air Force)

Raymond 'Bax' Baxter

Raymond Baxter was a qualified Spitfire pilot by the age of 18. His first operational posting was to No 65 Squadron, based in Scotland, flying Mk V Spitfires on shipping reconnaissance sorties. In early 1943 he was posted to North Africa, joining No 93 Squadron, a Spitfire Mk IX unit covering the First Army. After a year, he was sent home to instruct at No 61 Operational Training Unit. In September 1944 he returned to operational flying with No 602 Squadron. From Coltishall, in Norfolk, he flew Mk XVI Spitfires on ground attack missions, particularly dive-bombing V-weapon sites, including V-2 rocket launching pads. He was mentioned in despatches for his part in these raids. Having survived the war, Raymond Baxter carved out a very successful career as a broadcaster with the BBC, specialising in commentating on technical sports, such as motor cycling, rallying and motor racing, and also covering aviation and technology. He participated in many motor rallies himself, including 12 Monte Carlo rallies. In April 1999 Raymond Baxter opened the current BBMF Visitor Centre facility at RAF Coningsby. He died on 15 September 2006, aged 84.

Above: Spitfire TE311 starts up.

This picture: Spitfire XVI TD240 WX-V of No 302 Squadron.

FC
AIRSPACE

HURRICANE Mk IIC PZ865

Hurricane Mk IIC PZ865 was the last Hurricane ever built, from a total of 14,533. Fitted with four 20mm cannons and a Rolls-Royce Merlin XX engine, it came off the Hawker production line at Langley on 27 July 1944 with the inscription 'The Last of the Many' painted beneath the cockpit on both sides. It was test flown the same day by George Bulman, who had flown the maiden flight in the prototype Hurricane in 1935; he was, therefore, the pilot for the first flights of the very first and the last Hurricanes. In order to preserve it for posterity, the company purchased PZ865 back from the Air Ministry.

In 1950 PZ865 – wearing the civilian registration G-AMAU and a smart Oxford Blue and gold colour scheme – was entered in the King's Cup Air Race, sponsored by HRH Princess Margaret. Flown by Gp Capt Peter Townsend CVO DSO DFC and Bar, it achieved second place. Over the next three years the Hurricane participated in several other air races, being modified for racing with the removal of its cannons and the installation of two 'overload' wing fuel tanks.

Subsequently, PZ865 flew in various capacities under the ownership of Hawker Siddeley. By the 1960s, having been returned to its original camouflage colour scheme, PZ865 had become part of an unofficial collection of historic Hawker aircraft, which also included a 1924 Hawker Cygnet, a Hart and a Sea Fury, all based at the company's airfield at Dunsfold. The Hurricane made numerous appearances at air displays in the hands of company test pilots, including Bill Bedford OBE AFC and Duncan Simpson OBE. It was also flown for films including the epic movie 'Battle of Britain'.

In 1971, having been grounded for a while, PZ865 underwent a full refurbishment to flying condition. Then, in 1972, a combination of limited resources and restricted hangar space at Dunsfold led to Hawker Siddeley deciding that it could no longer maintain its collection of historic aircraft. Suddenly, Hurricane PZ865's future as a 'flyer' had become very uncertain indeed.

The intervention of Duncan Simpson, who was now the Hawker Siddeley Chief Test Pilot, and some astute manoeuvring behind the scenes, gained just sufficient permission for the Hurricane to be donated to the BBMF, which was then based at RAF Coltishall.

In March 1972, before anyone could change their minds, Duncan Simpson flew PZ865 to Coltishall and handed the Hurricane over to the Flight. His arrival with this precious piece of British aviation history was not expected. He was met by a BBMF flight sergeant who said, 'Afternoon Sir, what have we here?' Duncan replied, 'It's a Hurricane, flight sergeant, a very special Hurricane, and I'm handing it over to you. Look after it and make sure it's flying right into the future so that future generations can see it'.

For many years the aircraft appeared with the BBMF as 'The Last of the Many', but eventually the fabric bearing the inscription was removed and put on display in the BBMF headquarters. In 1996, replica 20mm cannons, funded by the Lincolnshire's Lancaster Association, were fitted to PZ865 to restore the aircraft's appearance to that of a Hurricane Mk IIC. PZ865 remains in the care of the BBMF, now based at RAF Coningsby, and Duncan Simpson's wish to keep the aircraft flying continues to be fulfilled.

Far left: PZ865 painted to represent Hurricane HW840/EG-S of No 34 Squadron as flown by Flt Lt Jimmy Whalen with South East Asia Command in 1944.

Left: PZ865 was the last Hurricane off the Hawker production line.

RF U
PZ865

Josef František

Josef František joined the Czechoslovakian Air Force in 1934. After Czechoslovakia was annexed by the Germans he joined the Polish Air Force, and fought with the Poles when Germany invaded the country in September 1939. He was shot down on 20 September 1939, but was rescued unharmed. When Poland was overrun he escaped and eventually reached France via an internment camp in Romania and North Africa. After the fall of France, František fled to Britain and on 2 August 1940 he was assigned to No 303 (Polish) Squadron, based at RAF Northolt, flying Hawker Hurricanes. The squadron was declared operational on 31 August and saw considerable action during the latter stages of the Battle of Britain. It is now recognised that No 303 Squadron was the highest scoring RAF unit during the Battle, despite being in action for only 42 days before it was withdrawn for rest on 11 October. František scored his first kill, against a German Bf 109E fighter, on 2 September 1940. During the following month he shot down 17 German aircraft and probably destroyed another; making him the fourth highest-scoring RAF pilot of the Battle. František was a talented but ill-disciplined pilot, who frequently broke formation, seemingly wanting to fight his own private war as a 'lone wolf'. The British commanding officer, Sqn Ldr Ronald Kellett, decided on a compromise and declared František a 'guest of the squadron', allowing him free rein. The next day he shot down three more enemy aircraft. On 8 October 1940, František's Hurricane crashed in Ewell, Surrey, in slightly mysterious circumstances, and he was killed at the age of 26. He was buried in the Polish military cemetery at Northwood. Josef František was awarded the DFM and Bar and several Polish honours including the Virtuti Militari Silver Cross.

Johnny Kent

Johnny Kent came from Winnipeg in Canada where he learned to fly and gained his commercial pilot's licence before he joined the RAF in 1935. After training, he served with No 19 Squadron at Duxford, flying Gloster Gauntlet biplanes, and then with the Royal Aircraft Establishment at Farnborough. For his research work there, during which he deliberately made over 300 airborne collisions with various types of barrage balloon cables, he was awarded an AFC. From May to July 1940 he flew unarmed Spitfires on photo-recce sorties over France. He then converted to the Hawker Hurricane and joined the newly-formed No 303 (Polish) Squadron as a flight commander on 2 August 1940. Flying with the squadron during the Battle of Britain he claimed three enemy aircraft destroyed and was subsequently awarded his first DFC. He was promoted to command No 92 Squadron in November 1940, flying Spitfires on offensive fighter sweeps over the continent, during which he destroyed three Bf 109s. In early 1941 he returned to Northolt to command the Polish Wing and quickly added three more Bf 109s to his score. Later, he was appointed to lead the Kenley Wing with whom he destroyed two further Bf 109s. His final total of wartime victories was 13 enemy aircraft destroyed, three probably destroyed and three damaged. In October he was awarded a Bar to his DFC. In 1942 he became the Station Commander at Church Fenton, before being posted to the Middle East. He returned to the UK in March 1944 and remained in the RAF after the war, enjoying a successful career and retiring in December 1956. He then became a sales manager with an aviation company. Johnny Kent died on 7 October 1985, at the age of 71.

Left: In its 'RF-U' colour scheme, PZ865 commemorated the exploits of No 303 (Polish) Squadron pilots and in particular those of Sgt Josef František.

Overleaf: Pilots of No 303 (Polish) Squadron, with Johnny Kent second from left.

'…a record unrivalled by any other squadron'

'It was with a very proud record that No 303 (Polish) Squadron left Northolt, the place of its rebirth, when we were moved north to Leconfield for a rest on 11 October 1940. In six hectic weeks the squadron had destroyed 126 enemy aircraft for the loss of only eight of our pilots killed, although a much greater number had suffered wounds of greater or less severity. It was a record unrivalled by any other squadron.

'František had been, perhaps, the most outstandingly successful of all the pilots in the squadron, destroying 17 of the enemy in a little over a month. His death came as a great shock to us all, it was totally unexpected and even now we do not know what actually happened. On 8 October, the squadron was returning to Northolt in formation, letting down in a shallow dive just over the Staines reservoirs when František pulled out and flew alongside the squadron… he turned slowly away to the east and disappeared. Sometime later we heard that he had crashed near Sutton and was dead when the rescuers got to the wreckage. He was seen approaching an open space apparently trying to make a forced-landing when suddenly his aircraft flicked onto its back and dived into the ground. We never did find out why this happened as we had not been in action and there were no bullet holes in either him or the aeroplane. It was not only a very great loss, it was a very worrying one.'

Group Captain 'Johnny' Kent DFC and Bar AFC Virtuti Militari
('Kentski' or 'Kentowski' to his Polish comrades) – Flight Commander No 303 (Polish) Squadron 1940

PZ865

Karel 'Kut' Kuttelwascher

Karel 'Kut' Kuttelwascher had amassed some 2,200 flying hours with the Czechoslovak Air Force before the Germans annexed his country in 1939. Three months later he escaped from Czechoslovakia to Poland, hiding in a coal train. He then made his way from Poland to France and was drafted into the French Air Force flying Morane-Saulnier MS406 and Dewoitine D.520 fighter aircraft during the brief but fierce Battle of France, claiming a number of German aircraft. When France fell, Karel escaped to Britain via Algeria and Morocco. He joined the RAF and was posted to No 1 Squadron just in time to earn his place as one of the 87 Czechoslovaks to fly with the RAF during the Battle of Britain. 'Kut' served for two years with No 1 Squadron. During the early 'circus' operations in 1941, he shot down three German Bf 109s and was credited with another as a 'probable'. On 1 April 1942 No 1 Squadron commenced night intruder operations from their base at RAF Tangmere. In a brief three-month period, on only 15 night missions, 'Kut' shot down 15 enemy bombers over their own bases in France (three in one night) and damaged a further five, earning himself a DFC and Bar. He also shot up several German 'E' boats and steam locomotives on nights when he had ammunition to spare on the way home. Remarkably, the rest of the war was relatively uneventful for him; whilst flying DH Mosquito night intruders he never even sighted another German aircraft. After the war had ended he returned briefly to Czechoslovakia but, in 1946, on the day that the communists effectively took control of his homeland, he flew back to Britain where he became an airline captain with British European Airways. He died prematurely in August 1959 from a heart attack, aged only 42.

Left: Top-scoring Hurricane night intruder ace Karel Kuttelwascher flew Hurricane IIC BE581 'JX-E'. PZ865 carried these marking to celebrate his achievements.

Below: Armourers reload the 20mm cannons of a No 1 Squadron Hurricane IIC.

Overleaf: A magnificent formation of No 1 Squadron Hurricanes in echelon.

JX B
JX I
JX

'I fired three short bursts'

'I took off well before midnight in bright moonlight and flew on a direct course from base to the target in France… On the almost blacked out aerodrome I spotted a plane with its navigation lights on. As he was taking off I dived after him and manoeuvred so that he was between me and the moon. He immediately switched off his navigation lights, but he was too late as he was already well placed in my gun sight. I fired three short bursts. There was no result from the first two, but after the third the aircraft turned steeply downwards and exploded on the ground. My plane rocked violently as if in a terrific gale. The enemy plane must have been loaded with bombs to have exploded like this and it gave me great satisfaction to know that he, at least, would never again deliver any of his loads on English soil.'

Flight Lieutenant Karel Kuttelwascher DFC and Bar
(Hurricane pilot with No 1 Squadron October 1940 to October 1942)

'…Left arm written off by cannon shell…'

'While on patrol over Luqa at 20,000ft, we were attacked from above and astern by six Me 109s [sic]. The Flight broke away to the right and formed a defensive circle. As I took my place in the circle I saw four more Me 109s coming down out of the sun. Just as they came within range I turned back towards them and they all overshot me without firing. I looked very carefully, but could see no more enemy aircraft above me, so turned back to the tail of the nearest 109. I was turning well inside him and was just about to open fire when I was hit in the left arm by a cannon shell. My dashboard was completely smashed. I baled out and landed safely by parachute.

'Our casualties: One Hurricane. Left arm written off by cannon shell. Shrapnel in both legs.'

Squadron Leader James 'Mac' MacLachlan DSO DFC and two Bars, Czech War Cross (Hurricane pilot with No 261 Squadron on Malta)

James MacLachlan

James 'Mac' MacLachlan flew Fairey Battle light bombers during the Battle of France in 1940 earning his first DFC. He then retrained on the Hurricane and flew with No 73 Squadron during the Battle of Britain, claiming a Bf 109 damaged. Having volunteered to go overseas, he led six Hurricanes to Malta off the deck of the aircraft carrier HMS *Argus* in the Mediterranean on 17 November 1940 as part of Operation 'White', the second such operation. On Malta he accounted for six Italian and German aircraft plus a 'damaged' and earned a Bar to his DFC before he was shot down on 16 February 1941 by a Bf 109. The injuries to his left arm were so severe that it had to be amputated. He was determined to get back to flying and once back in England he was fitted with a specially-designed artificial arm and was flying Hurricanes again by September 1941. On 3 November 1941 'Mac' was promoted squadron leader and given command of No 1 Squadron. Between April and June 1942, flying Hurricane Mk IICs on night intruder operations over France, he destroyed two enemy aircraft, damaged two more and shot up nine locomotives. He was awarded the DSO in May. In August 1942 he was posted to the Air Fighting Development Unit at Duxford, flying many different aircraft types. He claimed his final kills of the war in June 1943, flying a P-51 Mustang IA on a daylight long-range intruder mission. His final total score was 16½ destroyed, one probably destroyed and four damaged. On 18 July 1943 'Mac' was shot down by enemy ground fire whilst on another daylight intruder operation over France in a Mustang IA. He suffered severe head injuries when he crashed into a wood attempting to force land. He died in captivity 13 days later as a result of his injuries, aged 24. The second Bar to his DFC was gazetted after his death.

EG
S
PZ865

'...a tropical thunderstorm broke'

'Early in 1944, whilst at Palel, the squadron's Hurricane Mk IICs were fitted with bomb racks and the squadron converted to a fighter-bomber role. The 'Hurri-bombers' carried 2 x 250lb bombs armed with 11-second delay fuses so that attacks could be carried out at approximately 100ft. The bombing run was often followed by two strafing runs using the 4 x 20mm cannons. On one attack on a village in the Kabaw Valley called Kuntang things went wrong. Jimmy Whalen led the squadron and we had bombed and strafed the target and were forming up to return home when a tropical thunderstorm broke. The cloud base was down on the hilltops and there was no chance of climbing over the storm, but Jimmy led the 12 aircraft back to Palel with exceptional skill and when we were over the runway he said, "Get down as fast as you can". All the pilots were safe but two aircraft were written off and five others were unserviceable with flaps buckled by the water on the runway. The undercarriage of one Hurricane collapsed on landing and another landed in a paddy field 3/4 of a mile from the end of the runway... This operation left the Squadron with five serviceable aircraft and the ground crews worked like trojans to get us back on full readiness.'

Flight Lieutenant Jack Morton (sergeant pilot flying Hurricane Mk IICs with No 34 Squadron South East Asia Command)

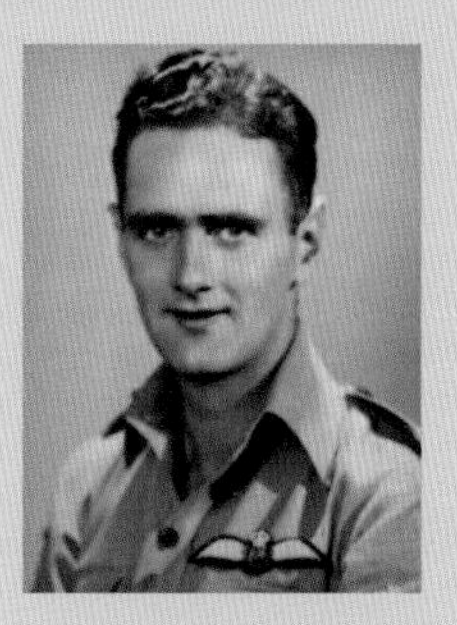

Jack Morton

Jack Morton joined the RAF on 6 July 1941. After completing his flying training in Britain and the USA, his first operational posting as a sergeant pilot was to the Far East where he joined No 34 Squadron, which had just converted from Bristol Blenheims to Hurricane Mk IICs and was now based at Cholaverum, near Madras, in India. He was allocated to 'B' Flight where the Flight Commander was Canadian Flt Lt Jimmy Whalen. After some weeks of intensive tactical flying the squadron was moved to Palel, a forward airstrip in the Imphal Valley. From there Jack Morton flew ground attack missions against the Japanese in Burma, in support of the Army. He flew 15 attacks in March 1944 alone. During the Battle of Kohima in April 1944 all the squadron's pilots were flying two or three times a day. The pilots had to contend not only with very dangerous Japanese fire from the ground but also unpredictable tropical weather. After the Japanese were defeated at Kohima and began their long retreat, the pace of operations did not let up. In October 1944, No 34 Squadron flew 859 ground attack sorties. By now Jack Morton had been commissioned and, when he left the squadron at the end of 1944, he held the rank of flight lieutenant and had personally flown 175 operational missions. He subsequently spent six harrowing months as a forward air controller, pursuing the Japanese Army through the jungles of Burma. Jack Morton returned to the UK in December 1945 and lived his life out in Scotland. He died on 16 October 2002.

'...I saw Jimmy roll over and crash'

'In the second half of April 1944 the Japs captured Kohima and it was decided to move 34 Squadron to an aerodrome in Assam at Dergaon. Life at Dergaon was hectic, all the pilots were flying two or three trips a day. On one very difficult target at the 'Rifle Range', Kohima, the Japs were holding up the Army and six of us were sent to help them. It was a difficult target to hit and I was flying as Jimmy Whalen's No 2, we went in to bomb in formation and dropped our bombs at 100ft. As we pulled up I saw Jimmy roll over and crash. Jimmy was easily the most popular pilot on the squadron and one of the best I ever flew with; 18 April 1944 was one of our blackest days.'

Flight Lieutenant Jack Morton (sergeant pilot flying Hurricane Mk IICs with No 34 Squadron SEAC and wingman to Jimmy Whalen when he was killed)

Jimmy Whalen

Jimmy Whalen enlisted in the Royal Canadian Air Force (RCAF) in June 1940, but was destined to fly with the RAF throughout his war. After completing his pilot training he was posted to England and joined No 129 Squadron. During fighter sweep operations over Europe in 1941 flying Spitfire Mk Vs, he shot down three Bf 109s (confirmed) and damaged another. In February 1942, he was posted to No 30 Squadron, which was embarking its Hurricane Mk IIBs on the aircraft carrier HMS *Indomitable,* to move them to Ceylon (now Sri Lanka). On 6 March, the Squadron flew off the aircraft carrier into Ratmalana, just outside Colombo. A Japanese naval strike force attacked Ceylon on 5 April 1942 with 125 carrier-based aircraft. In the ensuing, desperate aerial combats Jimmy Whalen destroyed three Japanese Navy 'Val' bombers (Navy type 99). In December 1942 he was transferred to No 17 Squadron in India. From then on, he flew Hurricanes in the fighter-bomber role against Japanese ground targets. In August 1943 he was posted to No 34 Squadron as a flight commander. On the morning of 18 April 1944, Jimmy led six of the squadron's Hurricane Mk IICs to attack a Japanese bunker on the Imphal-Kohima road. After he dropped his bombs, he was seen by his wingman, Sgt Jack Morton, to crash into the jungle. He was probably hit by enemy ground fire and either killed outright or incapacitated, such that his aircraft went out of control from very low altitude and crashed. He died just five days before his 24th birthday and had been recommended for the DFC two days earlier.

Previous spread: A spectacular photograph of a 'Hurri-bomber', with bombs just gone, making life very difficult for a Japanese vehicle in Burma.

Above: The sturdiness of the Hurricane made it ideal for operations in the Far East as a 'Hurri-bomber'.

Right: PZ865 as Flt Lt Jimmy Whalen's Hurricane, HW840/EG-S.

EG
S
PZ865

'...she's a sweet, bloody marvellous, wonderful kite!'

'Against the Japanese fighters our best chance in the Hurricane was to engage them from above, then dive away as steeply as possible... I must have dived vertically at full throttle for seven or eight thousand feet and when I tried to start easing out, I found there was nothing I could do. The controls were frozen solid ... It was obvious that baling out wasn't any good... there was only one thing left – the tail trim... I took one hand off the stick and wound the trim wheel back the merest fraction and then hauled on the stick with all my strength. I was rewarded by the faintest softness, the slightest yielding and bit-by-bit, repeating these actions, I knew I was going to be alright... until at length there was the horizon and I was flying straight and level... I looked at the airspeed indicator and I couldn't believe my eyes. How could I be doing only 300-odd miles per hour after that dive... The speed was dropping fast, as it should, throttled right back as I was. And then the penny dropped. I'd gone right round the clock not once but twice! I watched it absolutely fascinated, seeing it complete a counter revolution, pass down through 400mph on the inner scale and then through 240mph on the outer one... There was no doubt about it I thought, looking affectionately at the sturdy wings with their rows of rivets, she's a sweet, bloody marvellous, wonderful kite!'

Warrant Officer Terence Kelly (flew Hurricanes with No 258 Squadron against the Japanese in Singapore, Sumatra and Java during 1941-42)

Terence Kelly

Terence Kelly left England for Singapore in October 1941 and, as a sergeant pilot with No 258 Squadron, flew Mk IIA Hurricanes against the Japanese in Singapore, Sumatra and Java. When Java capitulated to the Japanese in March 1942 and with no means of evacuation, he became a prisoner of the Japanese for the next three and a half years. After seven months in a squalid prison he was transported to Japan with more than 1,000 fellow POWs in an ancient freighter. When he arrived in Japan he was taken to Habu, on Innoshima Island, and to a prisoner of war camp named Hiroshima 5. From this camp he was forced to work daily in the Hitachi Dockyard. He witnessed some of the American bombing of Japan, but was not aware of the atomic bomb being dropped on Hiroshima on 6 August 1945, even though it was only about 24 miles from the POW camp. The surrender of Japan was announced on 15 August 1945 and he began his journey home to the UK a month later. After the war, Terence became a quantity surveyor and set up offices in London and the Caribbean handling many different projects. His experiences led him to write his first novel and he became a full-time author, writing many more novels and plays for stage, television and radio. He also wrote several non-fiction books about his wartime experiences, including 'Hurricane over the Jungle'. His experiences as a POW in Japan had long-term consequences and in his later years he suffered from skin cancer, possibly as a result of working in the blazing sun, but most likely caused by radiation from the Hiroshima atomic bomb. He died in September 2013.

FLT LT PARKINSON
C
WK518

CHIPMUNK T10 WG486 & WK518

The two de Havilland Canada Chipmunks held on charge by the BBMF are the last in RAF service and are probably the least-seen aircraft of the fleet. They are used year-round primarily for the conversion and continuation training of BBMF fighter pilots on tail-wheel aircraft. Other functions include the reconnaissance of new venues, the delivery or collection of pilots and, occasionally, the delivery of small spare parts.

WG486

Chipmunk T10 WG486 was built at the de Havilland factory at Broughton, on Hawarden Airfield, near Chester, the same facility where the BBMF Lancaster PA474 was manufactured in 1945.

WG486 was delivered to the RAF in January 1952 and served with No 5 Basic Flying Training School, No 9 Refresher Flying School and No 2 Flying Training School (FTS) before being used by the Army Air Corps with Nos 651 and 657 Squadrons.

In December 1958, the aircraft was issued to No 114 Squadron in Cyprus, where it was used in operations against the EOKA terrorists, flying low-level reconnaissance patrols and convoy escort missions from Famagusta, Xeros and Akrotiri airfields, with British Army officers in the rear seat. The crisis ended in March 1959 and WG486 was brought back to the UK in 1961.

The aircraft returned to training flying for 16 years, with units that included the RAF College at Cranwell, Initial Training School at South Cerney and Church Fenton, No 1 FTS at Linton, Liverpool and Bristol University Air Squadrons and No 3 Air Experience Flight (AEF) at Bristol Filton.

In 1987 WG486 was moved to Germany to operate as part of the Gatow Station Flight in Berlin, which was then surrounded by Soviet Communist Block territory, where it embarked on a second phase of operational flying. For the next two years the Chipmunk was flown on what were then highly secret 'Cold War' covert photographic reconnaissance 'spying' flights in the zone around Berlin.

When RAF Gatow closed, the aircraft spent a year at RAF Laarbruch in Germany before joining the BBMF in 1995.

WK518

Also built at Broughton, Hawarden, and delivered to the RAF in January 1952, Chipmunk T10 WK518 has been with the BBMF the longer of the Flight's two Chipmunks.

WK518 has spent its life as a training aircraft. There must be literally hundreds of RAF flying instructors and student pilots who have delighted in the lightness and sensitivity of the Chipmunk's controls, and perhaps some students who struggled to master the tail-wheel landing idiosyncrasies.

Its initial service was with the RAF College at Cranwell where it was used for the elementary training of student pilots; other units which have operated WK518 include the University Air Squadrons (UASs) for Liverpool, Manchester, Cambridge, Hull, Leeds and London Universities.

Chipmunk WK518 was delivered to the BBMF from No 1 Air Experience Flight at Manston in April 1983 and has flown with the Flight ever since.

ROLLS ROYCE

KEEPING THE DREAM ALIVE

The Battle of Britain Memorial Flight (BBMF) is a regular Royal Air Force unit, manned by RAF personnel and funded by the Ministry of Defence. The Flight maintains 12 historic and irreplaceable aircraft in airworthy condition; aircraft that are, today, perhaps the most cared-for in the world, certainly maintained to a much higher standard than was possible during World War 2. The ongoing preservation of these priceless pieces of aviation heritage is planned on a long-term basis and is carried out with the ultimate aim of keeping the aircraft flying forever.

BBMF ENGINEERING TEAM

The BBMF Engineering Team, responsible for the maintenance of the Flight's fleet of historic aircraft, consists of just 30 RAF engineers, headed by the Flight's Engineering Officer (a squadron leader). He and his engineering management team of a warrant officer, flight sergeant, two Full Time Reserve Service (FTRS) chief technicians and three regular RAF sergeants, are responsible for engineering standards and safety on the Flight and for co-ordinating the servicing and maintenance programmes.

The other RAF technicians on the strength of the Flight form the 'Mechanical' Team and the 'Avionics' Team. The 'Mechanical' Team is the larger of the two and specialises in aircraft structures (including the airframes, flying controls, hydraulic and pneumatic systems) and the aircraft propulsion systems (including all aspects of the aircraft engines and propellers, fuel, oil, ignition and cooling systems). The smaller 'Avionics' Team is responsible for maintaining and, when necessary, upgrading all the electrical and avionics systems on the Flight's aircraft, ranging from simple emergency magnetic compasses to modern retro-fitted equipment, such as the Mode S IFF transponders, radios, GPS and traffic-alerting systems fitted to the aircraft.

The attractions of the unique, challenging and satisfying working environment of the BBMF mean that there is a long waiting list for regular RAF engineering personnel to be posted to the Flight. Everyone who joins this relatively small BBMF Engineering Team is a volunteer and the normal tour of duty with the Flight is three to five years. Sometimes, key NCO posts are occupied by engineers who have previously served on the BBMF and who have returned from the front-line for a second tour with the Flight, after being promoted.

Left: The mighty Rolls-Royce Merlin engine, the powerplant of the Spitfire, Hurricane and Lancaster.

Below: Engineers at the BBMF have to learn new skill sets when working on historic engines.

A small cadre of Full-Time Reservist (FTRS) technicians, embedded within the total of 30 engineers on the Flight, provides a core of experience in maintaining these historic aircraft. These FTRS engineers have many decades of experience with the BBMF between them, having served with the Flight for 20-30 years each.

ON THE JOB TRAINING

The engineering of the BBMF historic aircraft is very different from that of the modern front-line equipment of the RAF. For example, RAF 'Mechanical' technicians are now trained only on jet or turbo-prop engines, that being all that is required in the front-line. They receive no trade training at all on the piston engines that power all of the BBMF aircraft. With this in mind, the BBMF needs to train its engineers on the job in the 'old-fashioned' skills needed for the Flight's historic aircraft.

The Flight has a three-man Training and Standards Cell, consisting of a FTRS Chief Technician and two regular RAF corporals (from within the total of 30 technicians on the Flight), whose remit is to give engineers new to the Flight the best possible training to enable them to work safely and effectively on the BBMF's aircraft. The training provided by the Cell includes both academic instruction in relevant theory and also 'hands-on' technical training leading to specific engineering authorisations (qualifications) on the BBMF aircraft.

Every new arrival to the Flight's team of engineers is given formal, theory-based academic instruction, which includes the theory of basic piston engines and of the BBMF engine types, and the health and safety implications of maintaining the BBMF aircraft, focussing strongly on the safety issues associated with propellers and magneto ignition systems. The lack of redundancy and the paucity of back-up systems for the safety-critical components of aircraft of this vintage is also stressed. The BBMF may have the oldest aircraft in the RAF but the Flight is governed by exactly the same regulations as the rest of the RAF in terms of the training and qualifications to undertake various engineering tasks. The Flight's corporals provide this training and award specific engineering authorisations, such as the refuelling of aircraft and the correct procedure to prepare an aircraft for flight.

The BBMF Training Cell also runs trade qualification or 'Q' courses for both the 'Mechanical' and 'Avionics' technicians on the Flight, which, on successful completion of the examinations, entitle the tradesman to a RAF-wide 'competency' certification on the BBMF historic aircraft, valid for five years.

WHAT ABOUT SPARE PARTS?

This is a question often asked by visitors to the BBMF's hangar at RAF Coningsby, interested to know how the Flight manages to replace faulty or worn-out parts on its historic aircraft.

The BBMF has a healthy stock of spare parts held at its base at RAF Coningsby. These spares are controlled by a team of up to seven Supply personnel, both in the Supply Squadron itself and on the Flight.

Inevitably, not all the spare parts that may be needed are held at Coningsby; the long-term management and procurement of spares for the Flight is the responsibility of the BBMF Project Team. This small team of civil servants, contractors and a RAF Chief Technician is based at Coningsby and is responsible for maintaining the operating safety case for each aircraft, project managing the major maintenance contracts and implementing modifications to the aircraft.

In order to prevent the possibility of the Flight running out of certain critical spares, a meeting is held every six months to identify the items that, if not available, could potentially lead to aircraft being grounded. The BBMF engineering effort is supported by at least 18 small- or medium-sized companies around the country. These companies generally have a small but highly-skilled and dedicated workforce. They all hold the necessary accreditations that ensure they produce or overhaul spares to the required, standard. Most also supply the civilian 'warbird' community, and as such are required to hold the necessary Civilian Airworthiness Authority (CAA) accreditations. Additionally, spares are sometimes sourced via the Internet from the USA and Canada.

The combination of a good stock of spare parts and the ability to have parts made when required, ensures that the aim of keeping the BBMF aircraft flying forever will certainly not be prevented by a shortage of spares.

ENGINES

People often ask how the BBMF maintains the big piston engines for its aircraft and how the supply of engines and parts can be sustained almost 80 years after the first Rolls-Royce Merlins entered service with the RAF.

Although it means that they are no longer strictly authentic, most of the BBMF aircraft are not fitted with their original mark of engine. Driven by availability, ease of maintenance and management, and to enable the rationalisation of logistic support, the aircraft have been grouped together and modified where required to enable the use of common marks of engine as far as possible. The result is that today, the BBMF Spitfire Mk II and Mk V are powered by the Rolls-Royce Merlin 35 (instead of the original Mk XII and Mk 45); the Mk IX and XVI Spitfires both run the Packard Merlin 266 (which strictly speaking and confusingly makes the Mk IX a Mk XVI); the Mk XIX Spitfires are fitted with Rolls-Royce Griffon Mk 58 RG30 SM-S (modified Avro Shackleton engines), and the Hurricanes and Lancaster have Merlin 25, 225 or 500 engines which have a common build standard, configuration and power output.

With a pool of 17 Merlin and Griffon engines in total available to the BBMF, spare engines of the appropriate marks are usually readily available, on-hand, should an unscheduled engine change be required. This occurs infrequently with generally good reliability and it is not unusual for engines to reach their installed life limit which is now set at 500 flying hours (considerably less than the original limits). This is not a finite life though and at this point an in-depth reconditioning can be carried out which will allow the engine to be re-lifed for a further 500 hours.

Engine reconditioning work is not carried out by the Flight. The BBMF Project Team, responsible for managing all major maintenance contracts, currently utilises the services of a Gloucestershire based company, Retro Track and Air (UK) Ltd, to provide all its engine repair and overhaul facilities. In addition to completing full engine overhauls, the company also has the capability to manufacture components such as camshafts, pistons and running gear. In essence, if a technical drawing exists an item can be produced to the original manufacturer's specification, while pattern parts can also be made using reverse

Above: The Lancaster undergoing maintenance in the Flight's hangar.

Left: The very latest technology is combined with the old to keep the BBMF fleet airworthy.

Far left: The BBMF holds a healthy stock of spare parts for standard maintenance.

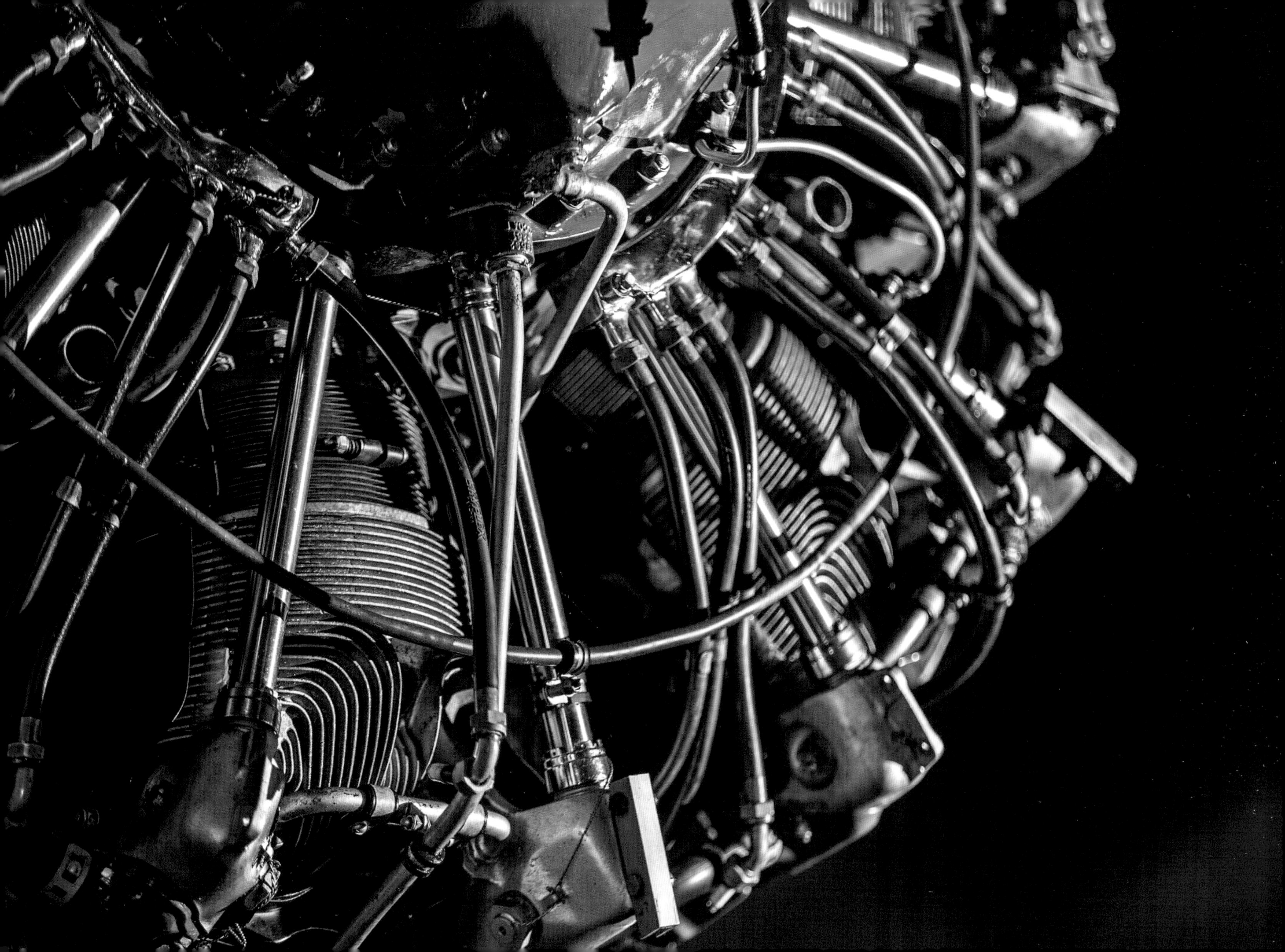

engineering techniques. On completion of an engine overhaul, the company carries out comprehensive testing using a custom-built dynamometer test bed, a procedure which identifies leaks or emergent faults and gives significant confidence in the product.

Clearly, engines are a critical item with regard to airworthiness, with no redundancy in terms of safety in the single-engine aircraft, so it is essential that they are maintained to the highest possible standards. Therefore, returning ageing components to an 'as new' condition is an ongoing requirement necessitating complex precision engineering processes. An example of this is the manufacture of brand new camshafts made to the original standards specified in drawings and original patterns. Existing camshaft profiles can also be cylindrically ground if repair is necessary, whilst specialist polishing or the application of advanced surface treatments can be applied to a wide range of precision parts including crankshafts.

It is not only the core engine components that require overhaul and refurbishment; there are a multitude of other engine ancillaries that require scheduled overhaul or repair, using an 'on condition' philosophy, including propeller Constant Speed Units and all fuel system components, such as carburettors and injection systems. This work is also carried out by 'Retro'. Meanwhile, the BBMF itself maintains magnetos to component level in-house. All of this ensures that a working asset level of serviceable engine ancillary components is readily available for use by the Flight.

MODERN REGULATIONS

In common with all British military aircraft, the historic aircraft of the BBMF are governed by the regulatory framework imposed by the Military Aviation Authority (MAA). Amongst these regulations is a requirement to 'baseline' all RAF aircraft back to 'birth', to confirm the airworthiness of each individual aircraft by establishing its maintenance history and physical configuration. Due to their age, it was impractical to check 'back to birth' for the BBMF aircraft, but as the Flight's aircraft have either undergone or will undergo a 'Major-plus' strip down and re-build, which provides the necessary evidence of each aircraft's standard, and confidence in their configuration, this was deemed to be an acceptable starting point.

In addition, each of the BBMF aircraft undergoes an annual Military Airworthiness Review, an independent check of each aircraft, carried out by a contracted company, and consisting of a comprehensive review of all the relevant documented aircraft records and a physical survey of the aircraft, leading to the award of a Military Airworthiness Review (MAR) certificate. Without a valid MAR certificate, the aircraft are not permitted to fly.

This process is identical to that applied to the most modern aircraft and is indicative of how the BBMF engineering has to be conducted to exactly the same standards and in accordance with the same regulations as all other RAF aircraft, regardless of the fact that the Flight's 'warbirds' are all over 70 years old. This compliance with modern regulations will ensure that the BBMF aircraft remain airworthy and fit for purpose well into the future.

Above: With cowlings removed, the interior of the Hurricane is revealed.

Left: Of the Flight's aircraft, only the Dakota has radial engines.

COMMEMORATING THE BATTLE

As part of the commemorations to mark the 75th anniversary of the Battle of Britain in 2015, the BBMF organised a 'meet' of Spitfires and Hurricanes at Coningsby for a unique formation. During that year, one of Coningsby's resident Typhoon fighters was painted to represent the No 249 Squadron Hurricane flown by Flt Lt James Nicolson on 16 August 1940. During his very first combat, Nicolson's aircraft was hit by four cannon shells fired by a Messerschmitt Bf 110, two of which wounded him whilst another set fire to the petrol tank in the nose of his aircraft, the flames spreading into his cockpit. He was about to bale out due to the flames when he sighted another enemy Bf 110. Retaking his seat he attacked it, although as a result of staying in his burning aircraft he sustained serious burns to his hands, face, neck and legs. For his courageous actions, Flt Lt James Nicolson was awarded the Victoria Cross, the only ever Fighter Command recipient. Such a high award for gallantry has to have witnesses and fortunately Nicolson's bravey was seen by people on the ground. Many other acts of selfless bravery took place in Fighter Command from 1939-45, but were out of sight of many. Such is the stark reality of battle joined in the extremes of altitude.

AIRCRAFT HISTORY & SPECIFICATIONS

SUPERMARINE SPITFIRE

The Spitfire design can be traced from the line of successful high-speed floatplanes designed by R. J. Mitchell and developed for the international Schneider Trophy races. In November 1934, the Board of Supermarine Aviation Works (Vickers) Ltd authorised Mitchell to proceed, as a private venture, with an entirely new fighter design to be powered by the Rolls-Royce PV12 engine (which later became the Merlin). This aircraft was the Spitfire. The maiden flight of the prototype Spitfire (K5054) took place on 5 March 1936 from Eastleigh Airfield, now Southampton Airport. The first production Spitfire (K9787) flew in May 1938 and the first Spitfires entered RAF service with No 19 Squadron in August 1938.

The Spitfire was produced in greater numbers than any other British combat aircraft before or since; 20,341 Spitfires (excluding the navalised Seafire versions) were built in 22 different variants, and the aircraft remained in production for 12 years. RAF Spitfires flew a total 835,000 operational sorties during World War 2 and Spitfires fought in virtually every operational theatre of the war and in many varied roles.

The development potential of R. J. Mitchell's design allowed the Spitfire to establish and then maintain the air superiority so vital to the defence of Britain and, subsequently, to keep pace with the improvements in performance of enemy fighters throughout World War 2.

The last operational sortie by an RAF Spitfire took place on 1 April 1954.

SPITFIRE Mk IIA SPECIFICATIONS

Wingspan:	36ft 10in (11.23m)
Length:	29ft 11in (9.12m)
Height (to top of propeller tips):	9ft 10in (3.02m)
Wing Area:	242sq ft (22.5m^2)
Maximum (operational) weight:	6,172lb (2,799kg)
Wing loading (fully loaded):	25.4lb/sq ft (122kg/m^2)
Engine:	Rolls-Royce Merlin XII of 1,135bhp (at 12,250ft)
Propeller:	Rotol 3-bladed constant speed
Maximum level speed:	354mph (at 17,550ft)
Rate of climb:	2,995ft/min (at 10,000ft)
Service ceiling:	36,500ft
Maximum internal fuel:	85 Imp gal
Maximum combat range:	400 miles
Armament:	8 x 0.303in Browning machine guns

HAWKER HURRICANE

The Hawker Hurricane was at the forefront of Britain's defence in 1940 and played a major part throughout World War 2. A remarkable 14,533 Hurricanes were built and the aircraft served operationally on every day of the War, in every operational theatre and in many roles.

Hawker's Sydney Camm began the design work for the Hurricane in 1934 and the prototype Hurricane (K5083) made its maiden flight on 6 November 1935 from Brooklands Aerodrome, with Hawker's Chief Test Pilot, George Bulman, at the controls. The first production Hurricane (L1547) flew on 12 October 1937 and deliveries to the RAF commenced just before christmas 1937. The Hurricane was the first British monoplane eight-gun fighter, the first RAF aircraft to exceed 300mph in level flight and the first production fighter with a retractable main undercarriage.

When the Battle of Britain commenced in July 1940, RAF Fighter Command fielded 30 Hurricane squadrons compared with 19 Spitfire squadrons, and it is well known that Hurricanes achieved a higher proportion of combat kills during the Battle. The Hurricane's robustness, perhaps epitomised most by its ability to operate reliably from rough air strips in the desert or jungle, endeared it to all those associated with it.

The last Hurricane ever built, Mk IIC PZ865, was named *The Last of the Many* when it emerged from the production line at Langley on 27 July 1944.

HURRICANE Mk IIC SPECIFICATIONS

Wingspan:	40ft 0in (12.19m)
Length:	32ft 3in (9.82m)
Height (to top of propeller tips):	13ft 3in (4.04m)
Wing Area:	258sq ft (23.97m^2)
Maximum (operational) weight:	8,044lb (3,648kg)
Wing loading (fully loaded):	31.2lb/sq ft (152.3kg/m^2)
Engine:	Rolls-Royce Merlin XX of 1,280bhp (at 17,500ft)
Propeller:	de Havilland or Rotol 3-bladed constant speed
Maximum level speed:	340mph (at 21,000ft)
Rate of climb:	2,750ft/min
Service ceiling:	36,000ft
Maximum internal fuel:	94 Imp gal (plus optional 2 x 45gal drop tanks)
Combat range:	460 miles (extendable with drop tanks)
Armament:	4 x 20 mm Hispano cannons (91 rounds per cannon), 2 x 250lb or 2 x 500lb bombs

AVRO LANCASTER

The Avro Lancaster was the most famous and successful RAF heavy bomber of World War 2. Between 1941 and early 1946 a total of 7,377 Lancasters were built, at a 1943 cost of approximately £50,000 each. Some 3,249 Lancasters were lost in action from the 6,500 that flew on 'ops' during World War 2.

Designed by Avro's chief designer, Roy Chadwick, as an evolution of the troublesome Manchester, the prototype Lancaster took to the air for its first flight from Manchester's Ringway Airport on 9 January 1941.

The majority of Lancasters were fitted with four Rolls-Royce Merlin engines, but 300 Lancaster BIIs were built with Bristol Hercules radial engines.

With its 33ft (10m) long, unobstructed bomb bay, the Lancaster could carry the largest bombs used by the RAF, including the 4,000lb, 8,000lb and 12,000lb HC 'blockbuster' blast bombs, often supplemented with smaller bombs and incendiaries. The Lancaster could also carry the remarkable 12,000lb 'Tallboy' and 22,000lb 'Grandslam' 'earthquake' bombs, designed by Barnes Wallis, for use against 'hardened' targets.

By the end of the war in Europe in May 1945, Lancasters of RAF Bomber Command had flown 156,000 operational sorties and dropped well over 600,000 tons of bombs.

The Lancaster is one of the icons of British aviation; the heavy bomber most associated with the RAF night offensive over Germany, .

LANCASTER B1 SPECIFICATIONS

Wingspan:	102ft 0in (31.09m)
Length:	69ft 4in (21.11m)
Height:	20ft 6in (6.25m)
Wing Area:	1,297sq ft (120.5m^2)
Maximum (operational) weight:	68,000lb (30,909kg) normal maximum loaded weight
Engines:	4 x Rolls-Royce Merlin XX of 1,280bhp each
Maximum speed:	282mph at 63,000lb (28,576kg) all up weight and 13,000ft
Rate of climb:	720ft/min at 63,000lb (28,576kg) all up weight and 9,200ft
Service ceiling:	21,400ft at 63,000lb (32,659kg) all up weight
Maximum fuel:	2,154 gal
Maximum range:	2,500 miles (4,023km)
Defensive Armament:	8 x 0.303 Browning machine guns
Bomb Load:	Maximum normal bomb load 14,000lb (6,300kg)
Crew:	Normally 7 (pilot, flight engineer, bomb aimer, navigator, wireless operator, mid-upper gunner and rear gunner)

DOUGLAS C-47 DAKOTA

The C-47 Dakota was a product of the Douglas Aircraft Company and is generally regarded as the best military transport aircraft of World War 2. It saw widespread service with the Allied air forces during the war and subsequently with air forces and civilian operators worldwide.

The first flight of the Douglas DC-3 airliner, from which the military transport version evolved, took place on 17 December 1935. Deliveries of the C-47 commenced in October 1941. Over 10,000 DC-3s and C-47s were built in total, most being C-47s. The Dakota's amazing ruggedness became legendary and its capabilities were increased to permit it to carry a freight payload more than double the original specification.

The first Dakota, as the aircraft became known in RAF service, was delivered to the RAF in 1942. The Dakota III eventually equipped 22 RAF squadrons and three RCAF squadrons under RAF operational control. In all, over 1,900 Dakotas were delivered to the RAF. As a tactical transport aircraft, the Dakota was used to carry troops and freight, for the air-dropping of supplies and paratroopers, for towing gliders and for casualty evacuation. Dakotas served in every theatre of the war, most notably in Burma and during the Allied airborne landings on D-Day, at Arnhem and the crossing of the Rhine.

Its work was, perhaps, often unglamorous and largely 'unsung' but the C-47 Dakota and its crews played a crucial role in the final Allied victory of World War 2.

C-47 DAKOTA III SPECIFICATIONS

Wingspan:	95ft 6in (29.41m)
Length:	63ft 9in (19.43m)
Height:	17ft 0in (5.18m)
Wing Area:	987sq ft (91.70m^2)
Maximum (operationa) weight:	29,000lb (13,150kg)
Max Overload:	31,000lb (14,060kg)
Engines:	2 x Pratt & Whitney Twin Wasp R-1830-90C 14-cylinder radials of 1,2008bhp each
Propellers:	Hamilton Standard, 3-bladed, full-feathering, constant speed
Maximum speed:	224mph (at 10,000ft)
Service ceiling:	24,000ft
Maximum fuel:	670 Imp gal (plus 80 gal in long range tank if required)
Maximum range:	3,800 miles (5,795km)
Maximum freight payload:	6,000lb (2,700kg) or 28 paratroopers or 14 stretcher patients
Crew:	Usually 3 (pilot, co-pilot, navigator/wireless operator)

FLIGHT HERALDRY

Until 1977 the Royal Air Force Battle of Britain Memorial Flight (RAF BBMF) had no official badge of its own. The Officer Commanding the BBMF at that time was Sqn Ldr Ken 'Jacko' Jackson MBE AFC. He had decided that the Flight should have its own 'proper' badge and he started a competition for a winning design. Mr Stuart Stephenson MBE, the then chairman of the Lincolnshire's Lancaster Association, which supports the Flight, submitted a design which eventually became the official badge.

The BBMF badge has the black silhouettes of a Lancaster, Hurricane and Spitfire flying in formation at an angle, superimposed over the centre of an RAF red, white and blue roundel. The full title 'Battle of Britain Memorial Flight' did not fit round the top, so the badge simply carries the name 'Memorial Flight'. The unit's motto 'Lest We Forget' was something Stuart Stephenson saw on a war memorial whilst stuck in a traffic jam one day; he thought it would do nicely.

'Jacko' Jackson liked the design and adopted it immediately and initially without official approval. Eventually, however, the badge received the necessary official approval from the College of Arms and Her Majesty The Queen provided Royal approval by signing the hand-painted original in 2002.

BBMF CHRONOLOGY

11 July 1957	Historic Aircraft Flight forms at RAF Biggin Hill with one Hurricane (LF363) and three Spitfire PR Mk XIXs (PM631, PS853 and PS915).
September 1957	Spitfire PR Mk XIX PS915 grounded until 1986.
October 1957	Three Mk XVI Spitfires join the Flight (TE330, TE476 and SL674).
February & March 1958	Flight's name officially changed to Battle of Britain Flight. RAF Biggin Hill closes. Flight moves to RAF North Weald.
April 1958	Spitfires PR Mk XIX PS853 leaves the Flight (rejoins in 1964).
May 1958	RAF North Weald closes. Flight moves to RAF Martlesham Heath.
September 1959	Two Spitfire Mk XVIs (TE476 and SL674) retired from service due to accidents. Spitfire XVI TE330 donated to the Smithsonian Institute, Washington DC.
November 1961	Flight moves to RAF Horsham St Faith.
April 1963	Flight moves to RAF Coltishall.
1965	Flight acquires Spitfire Mk Vb AB910 from Vickers Armstrong.
1968	Flight acquires Spitfire Mk IIa P7350 after the making of the film 'Battle of Britain'.
1969	Flight's name changes to Battle of Britain Memorial Flight.
1972	Flight acquires Hurricane Mk IIC PZ865 from Hawker Aircraft.
1973	Flight acquires Lancaster B1 PA474 from RAF Waddington.
1976	Flight moves from RAF Coltishall to RAF Coningsby.
April 1983	Flight acquires Chipmunk T10 WK518 (ex-RAF Manston).
1985	Flight acquires DH Devon VP981 (retired 1993, sold 1997).
April 1987	Spitfire PR Mk XIX PS915 returns to the Flight after refurbishment by BAe.
September 1991	Hurricane LF363 out of service due to an accident, awaiting re-build.
July 1993	C-47 Dakota ZA947 acquired (ex-Boscombe Down).
June 1994	Spitfire PR Mk XIX PS853 sold (now operated by Rolls-Royce) to defray costs of rebuild on Hurricane LF363.
June 1995	Flight acquires Chipmunk T10 WG486 (ex-RAF Gatow, Berlin).
November 1997	Flight acquires Spitfire Mk IX MK356 (ex-St Athan Museum collection).
September 1998	Hurricane LF363 returns to service after rebuild.
2000	Flight granted semi-autonomous status as an independent supported unit.
April 2002	Two non-flying Spitfire XVIs (TE311 and TB382) allocated to BBMF for spares support. TB382 dismantled for spares and struck off charge. TE311 rebuild to airworthy status commences.
October 2012	Spitfire Mk VXI LFe TE311 flies for the first time in 58 years. The Flight now operates six Spitfires.

Acknowledgements

A work such as this is only made possible through the passion, assistance, persistence and the imagination of many individuals. John Dibbs would like to thank, Iain Dougall, Clive Rowley, George 'Johnny' Johnson, Allan Burney, Phil Hempell, Kent Ramsey, and Pam Dibbs. I'd also like to thank Jim, Bob and Scott Donovan at Kenmore Camera and Mike Gurley at Canon for their technical advise and support. We did it!

Many thanks also to the Royal Air Force and The Battle of Britain Memorial Flight, the pilots, engineers, admin and Media Comms support that makes this unique and important Squadron the envy of the World's air forces. All their hard work has and will allow past, current and future generations to experience the sight and sound of a Spitfire, Hurricane, Lancaster or Dakota, keeping them a reality of bygone sacrifices in our skies. I am grateful to the incumbent OCs during my work with the Flight, Sqn Ldr Al Pinner, Sqn Ldr Dunc Mason and Sqn Ldr Andy Millikin as well as the ever-present and enthusiastic Flt Lt 'Parky' Parkinson and Air Cdre Jez Attridge.

Camera ship pilots who flew brilliantly for the project were Tim Ellison, Will Gray, Peter Monk and Richard Verrall.
Thanks also to RAF Coningsby's talented photo-section for the stunning engineering and ground operation images. Photo credits are also due to Chris Elcock (page 118), Colin Smedley (page 106) and the Key Archive, from which many of the black and white images were sourced. The colour images on pages 10 and 105 © IWM.

I must express my gratitude to Adrian Cox, Ann Saundry and Nigel Price at Key Publishing for joining in the vision to create this book. Iain Dougall for his enthusiasm, support and invaluable assistance on the project. Allan Burney worked many unsociable hours to help me create this work and to him I am indebted for his friendship and resilient spirit. Thanks also to Brian Denesen at The Plane Picture Co for his support and work ethic. A special mention for Clive Rowley who's passion and professionalism proved to be a source of inspiration.
Pam Dibbs helped me to create a strategy to realize this important project, and gave me the belief to follow my heart and enable it to happen. I am indebted to you all.

Bibliography

These books have provided inspiration and some research material for this book:'Spitfire – A Test Pilot's Story' by Jeffrey Quill published by Air Data Publications 1996. 'Gun Button to Fire' by Tom Neil published by Amberley Publishing 2010. 'They Called Me Dixie' by Captain Richard L. Alexander published by Robinson Typographics 1988 (out of print). 'One Man Air Force' by Captain Don S. Gentile as told to Ira Wolfert (out of print). 'The Darlington Spitfire – a charmed life' by Peter Caygill (Airlife Publishing Ltd 1999). 'Wing Leader' by Air Vice Marshal 'Johnnie' Johnson published by Air Data Publications Ltd 1995. 'Spitfire Offensive' by Wing Commander R. W. F. Sampson with Norman Franks published by Bounty Books 2007. 'Sky Spy' by Ray Holmes published by Airlife Publishing Ltd 1989. 'One of the Few – A Triumphant Story of Combat in the Battle of Britain' by Johnny Kent published by The History Press Limited 2000 & 2008. 'Night Hawk' by Roger Darlington published in 1985 by William Kimber & Co Ltd. 'Hurricane over the Jungle' by Terence Kelly published by Leo Cooper Ltd (new edition March 2005). 'Fighter Pilot' by Paul Richey, first published 1941 by B.T. Batsford Ltd and re-printed many times. 'Operation "BOGRAT" – From France to Burma' by Donald Stones first published in the UK in 1990 by Spellmount Ltd. 'Flying Scot – An Airman's Story' by Air Commodore Alastair Mackie CBE DFC published by Pen and Sword Aviation in 2012. 'Drop Zone Burma – Adventures in Allied Air Supply 1943-45' by Roger Annett published by Pen and Sword Aviation in 2008. 'Follow your Leader – a Biography of Wing Commander Peter Bailey' by Jennifer Margaret Simpson (limited edition book, published privately in Australia). 'Ploughshare and Shining Sword – a biography of John Chatterton DFC MSc' by Richard W Underwood, published by Tucann Design & Print in 2004. 'No Moon Tonight' by Don Charlwood, first published in 1956, published in UK by Goodall Publications UK in 1984. 'Boys at War' by Russell Margerison, published by Northway Publications; 2nd new edition 2005. 'A Tail End Charlie's Story' by H. James Flowers, published privately with all proceeds donated to the International Bomber Command Centre in Lincoln.

AUTHOR'S NOTE: The ranks and decorations given for all of the individuals quoted in this book are the final ranks and decorations they achieved, rather than those they held at the time of the incident they describe. The individual aircraft are listed in chronological sequence under date of entering service.

LEST WE FORGET